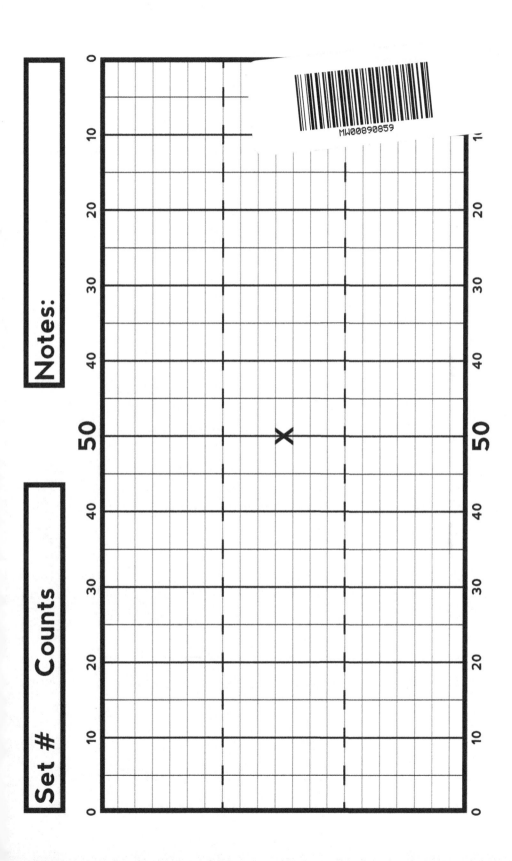

Set #   Counts   Notes:

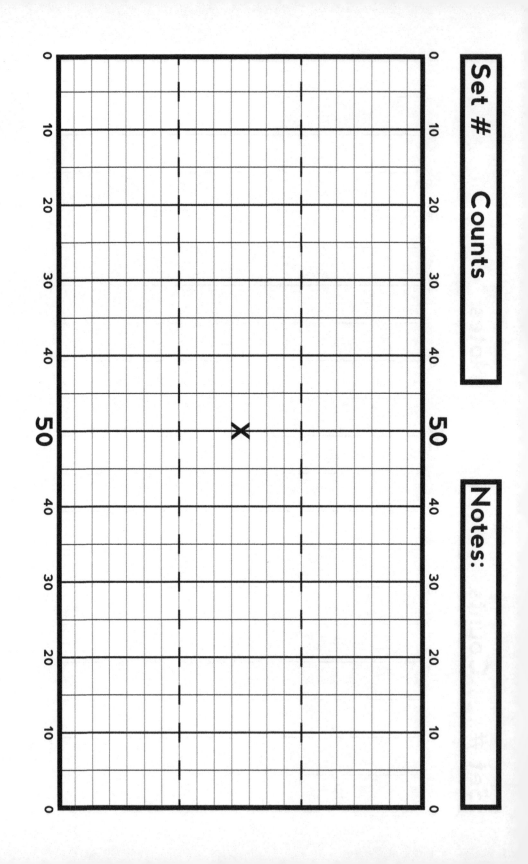

Set #

Counts

Notes:

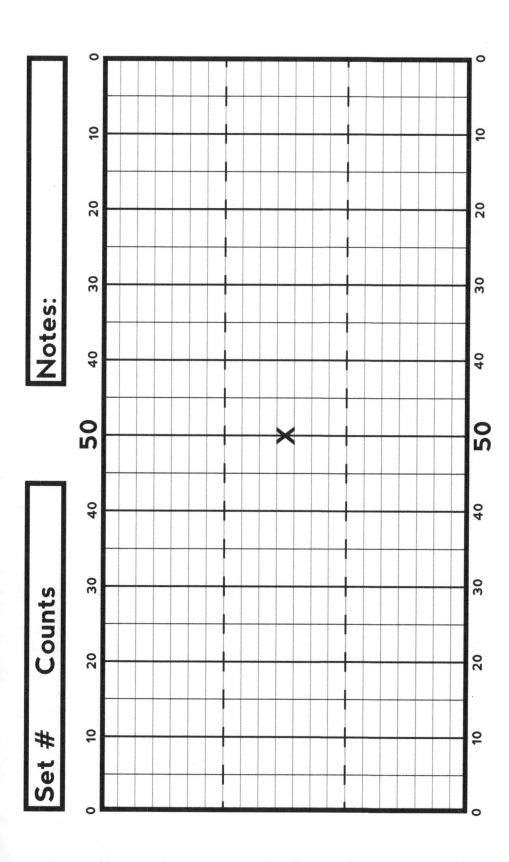

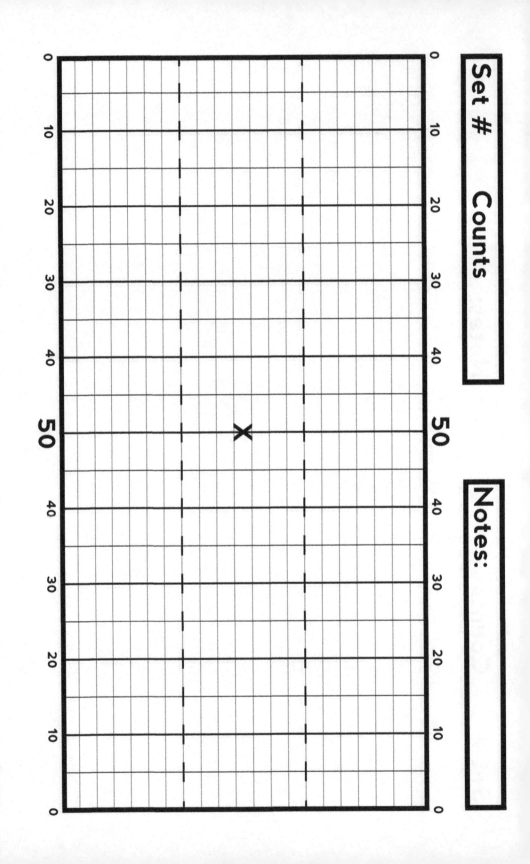

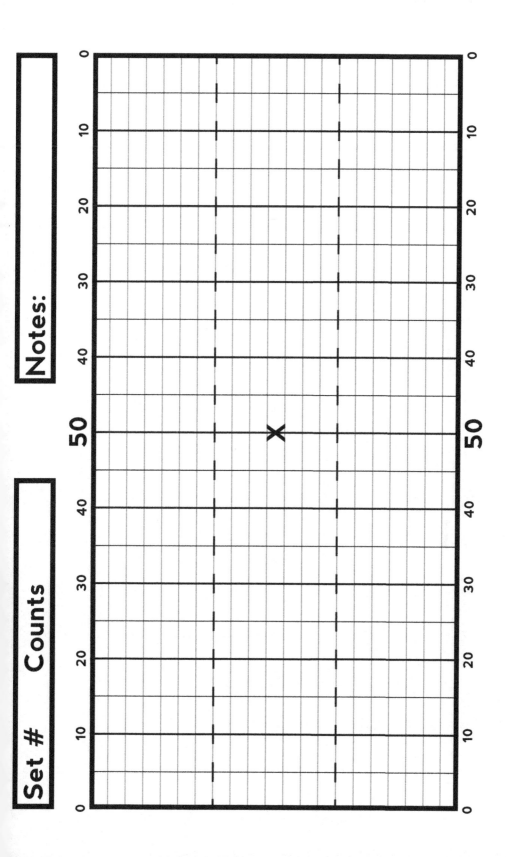

Set # ____ Counts ____ Notes: ____

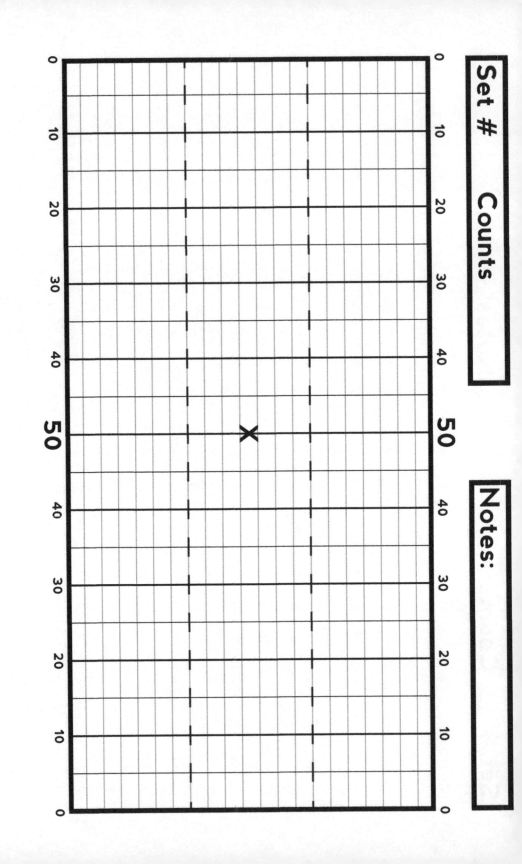

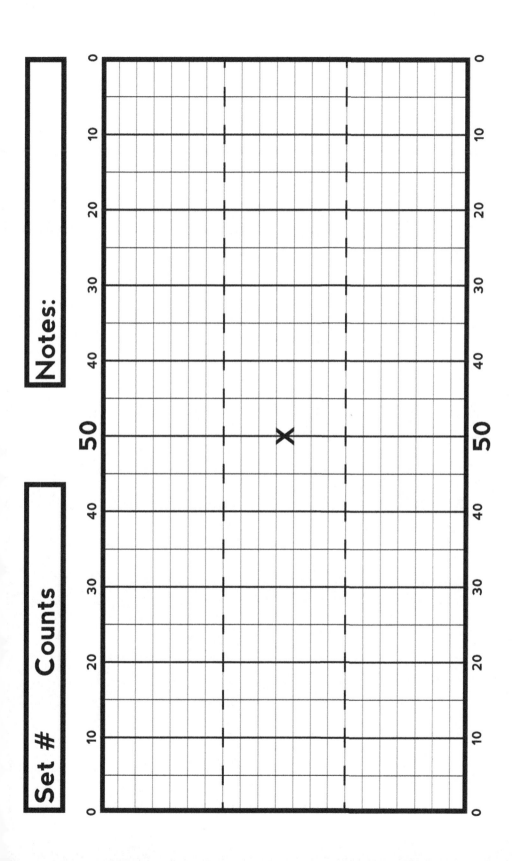

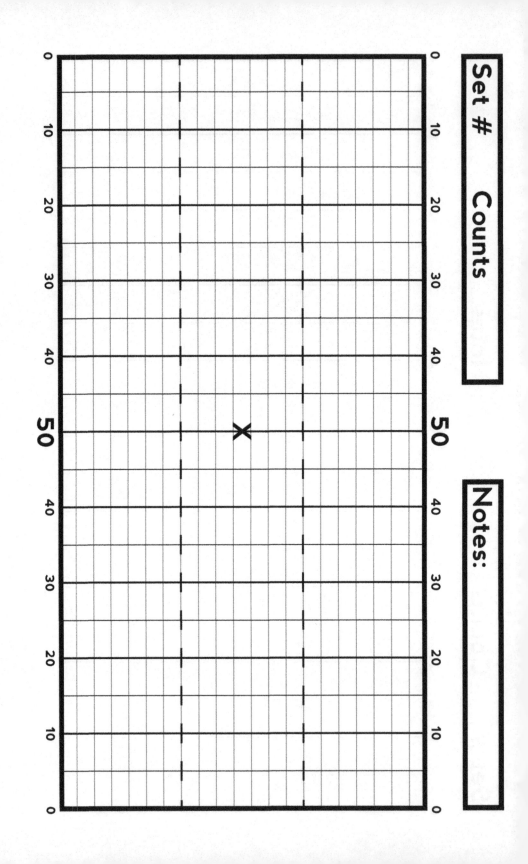

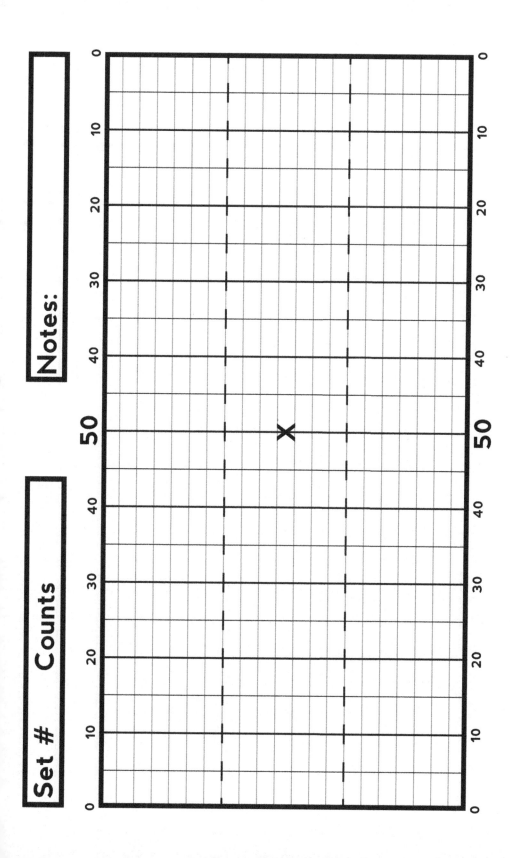

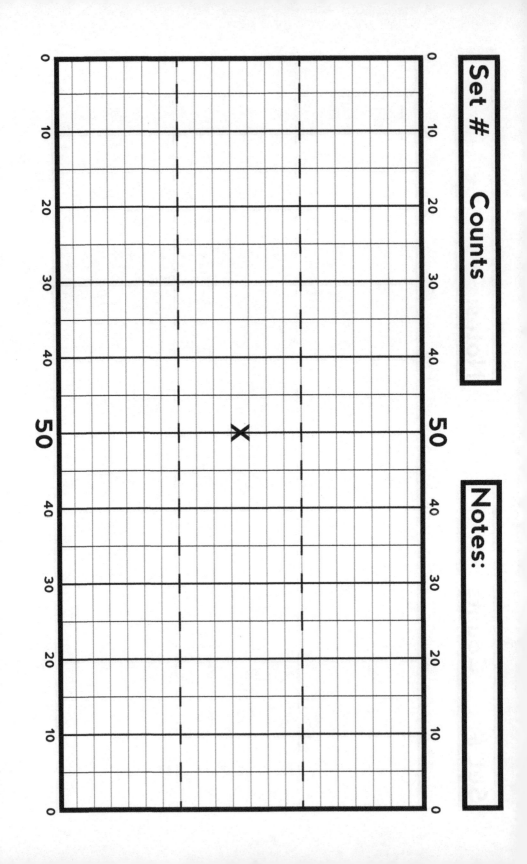

Set #   Counts   Notes:

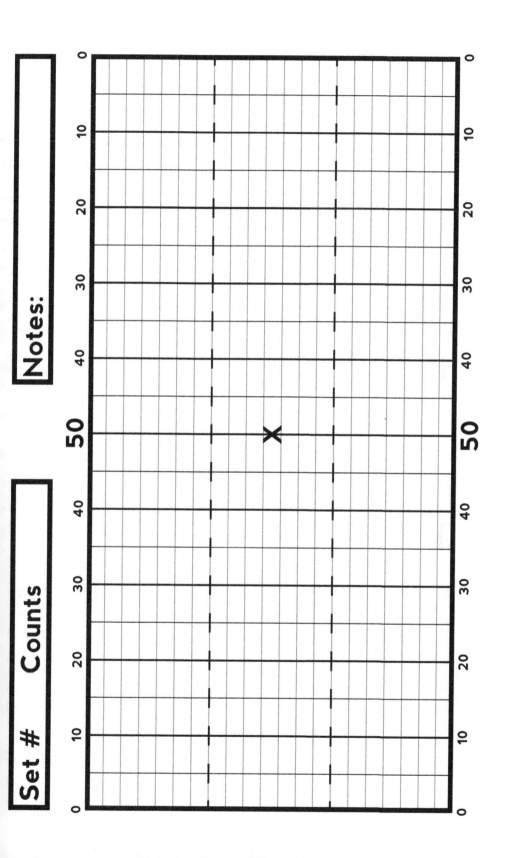

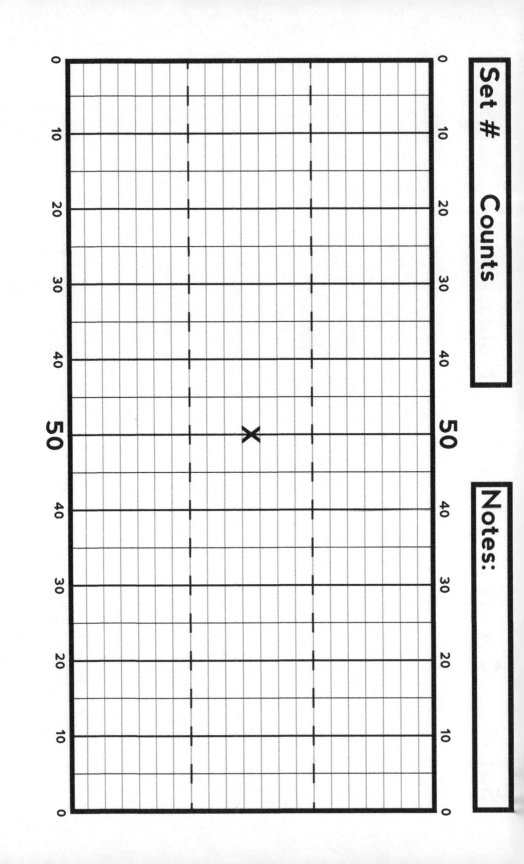

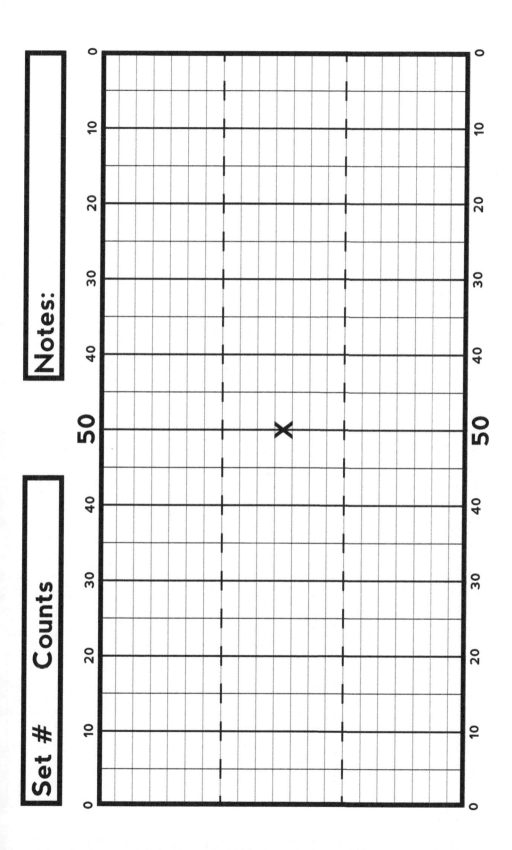

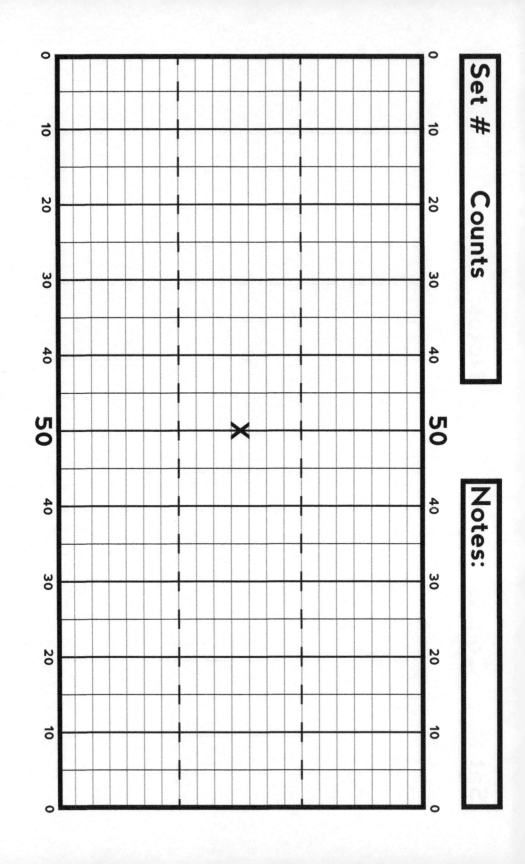

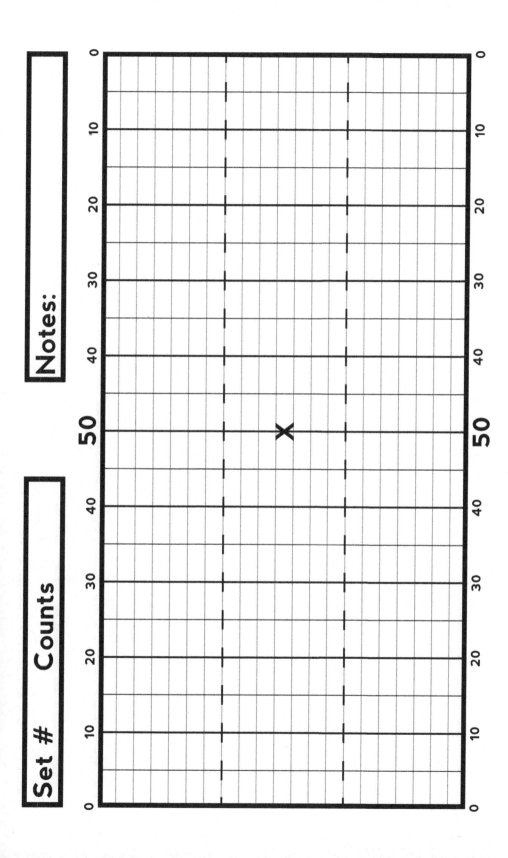

Set #　　Counts

Notes:

Counts Notes:

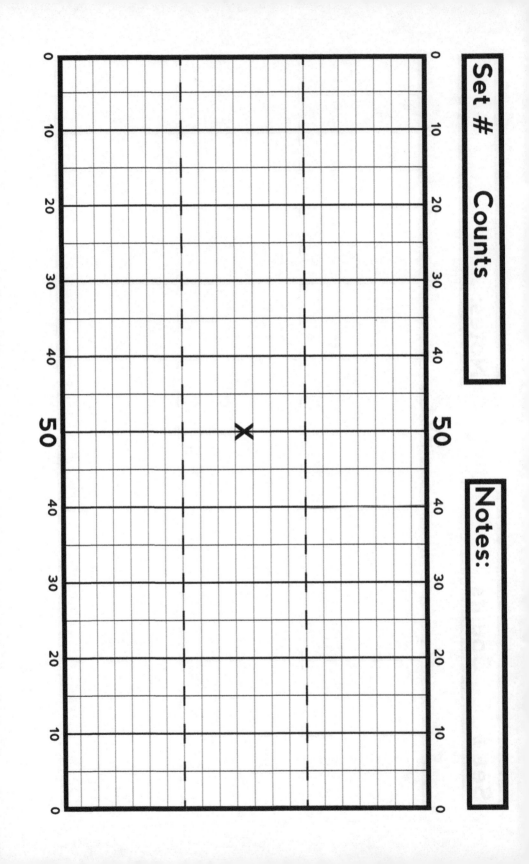

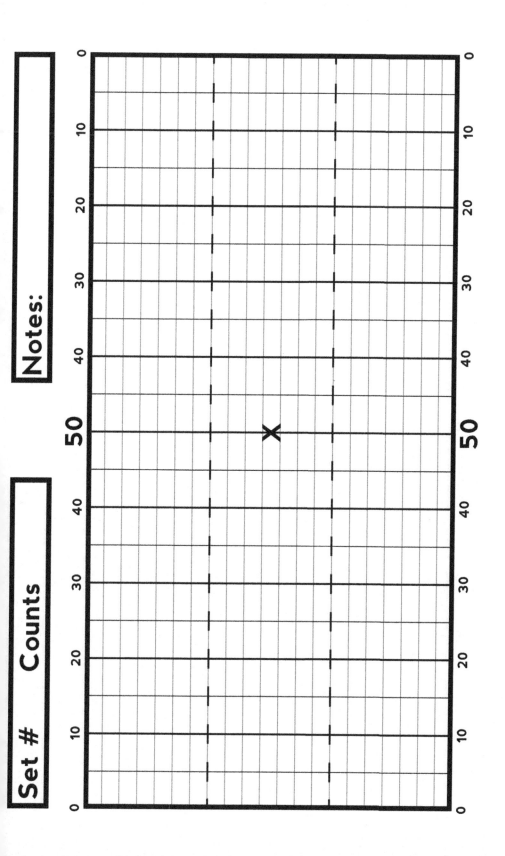

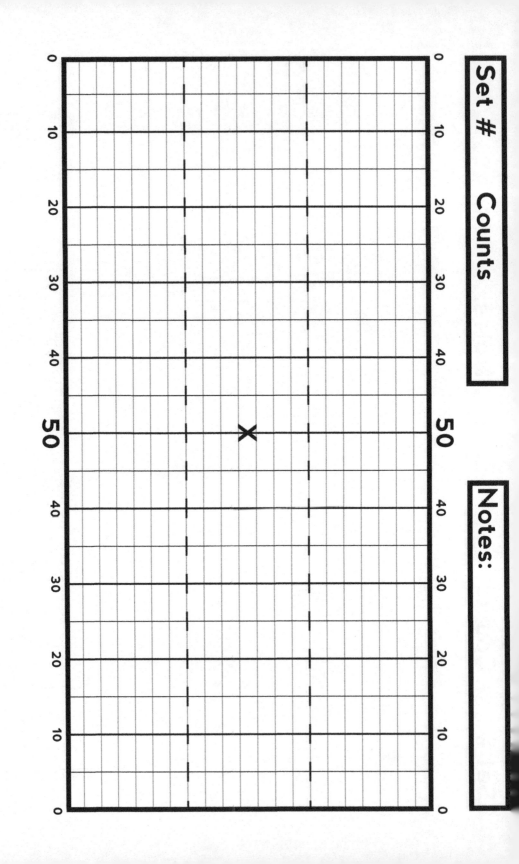

Set #   Counts

Notes:

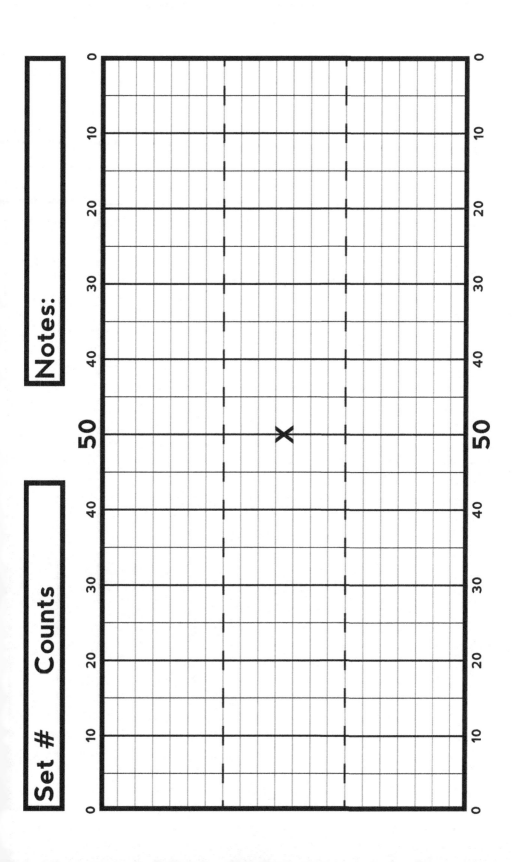

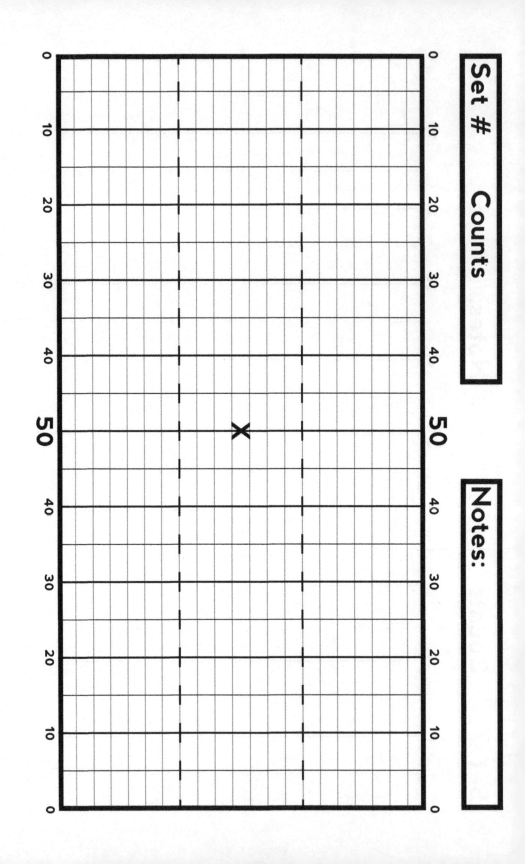

Set # Counts

Notes:

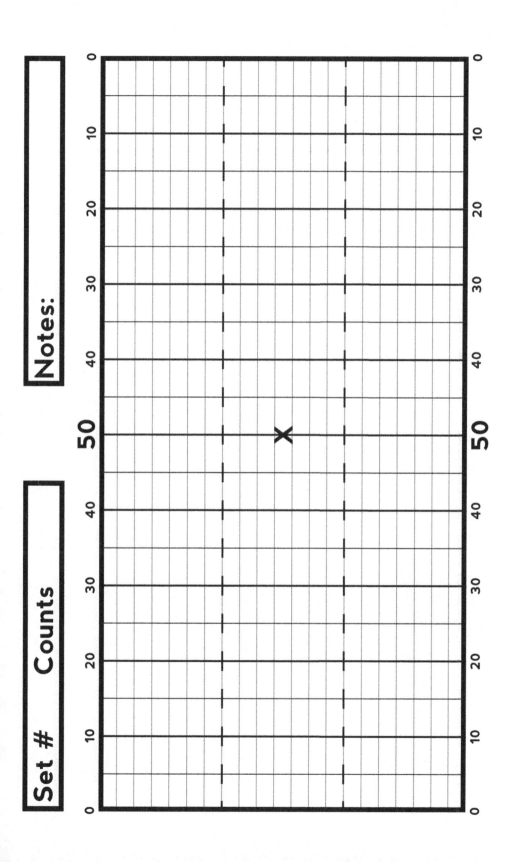

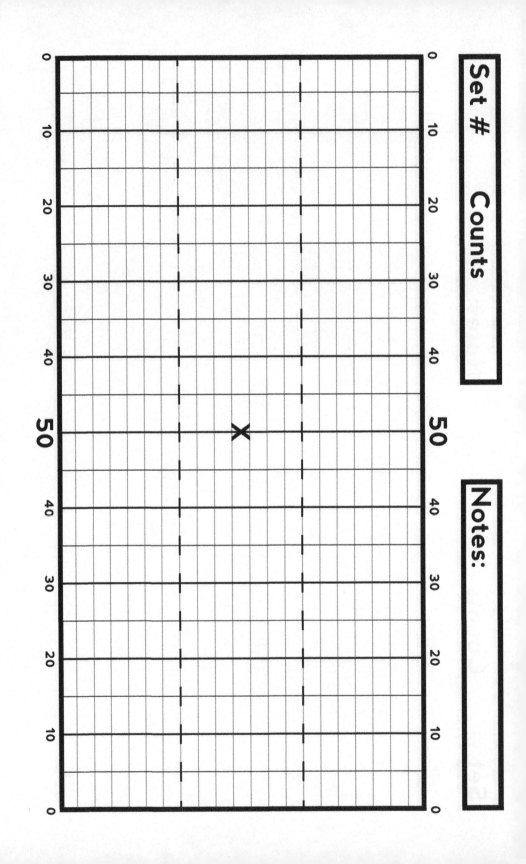

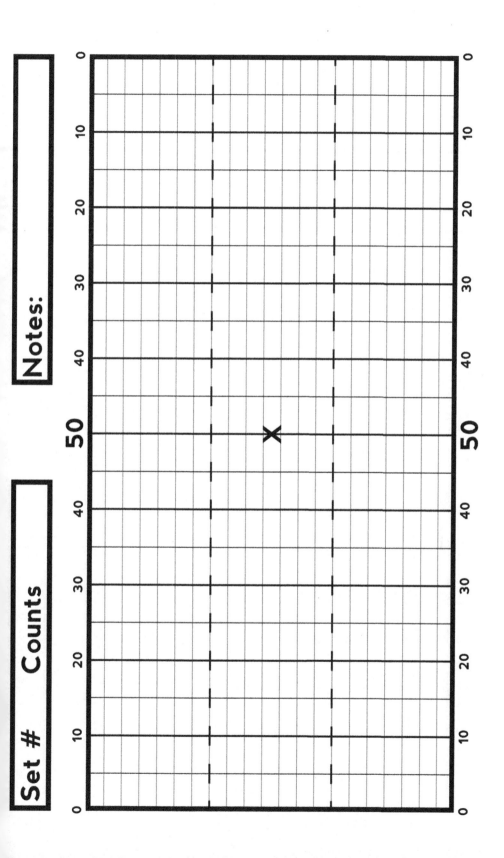

Set # _____ Counts

Notes:

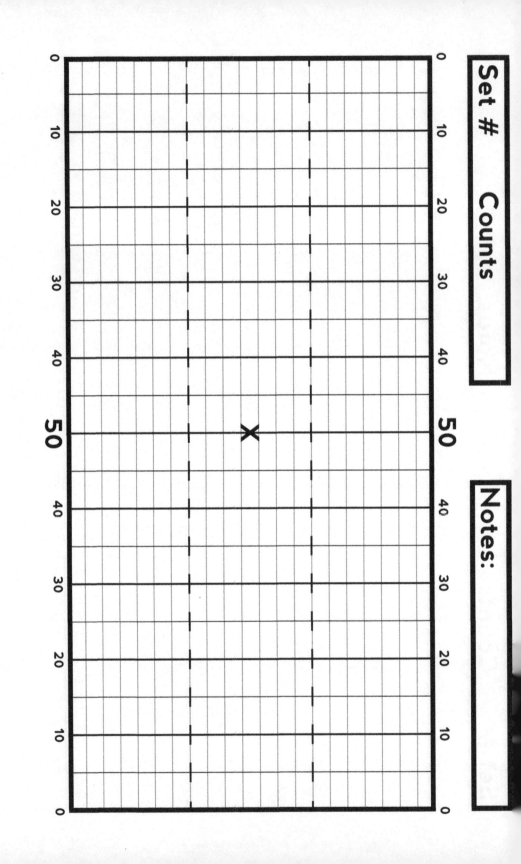

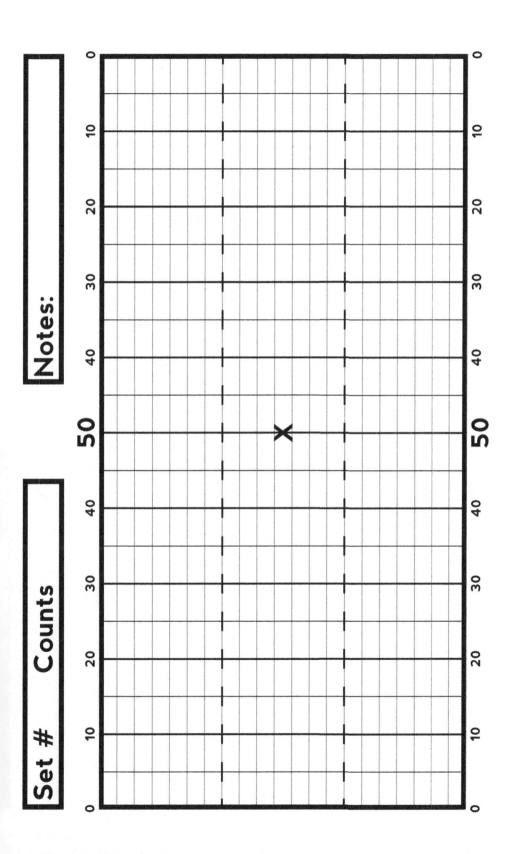

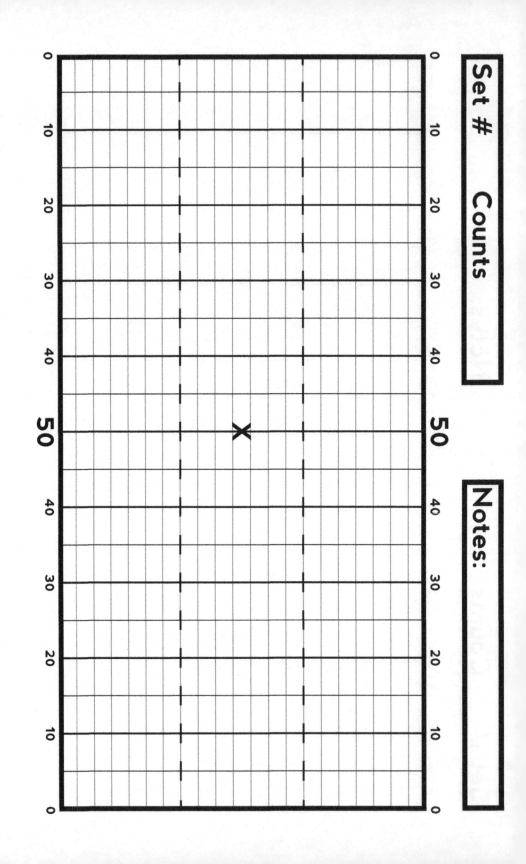

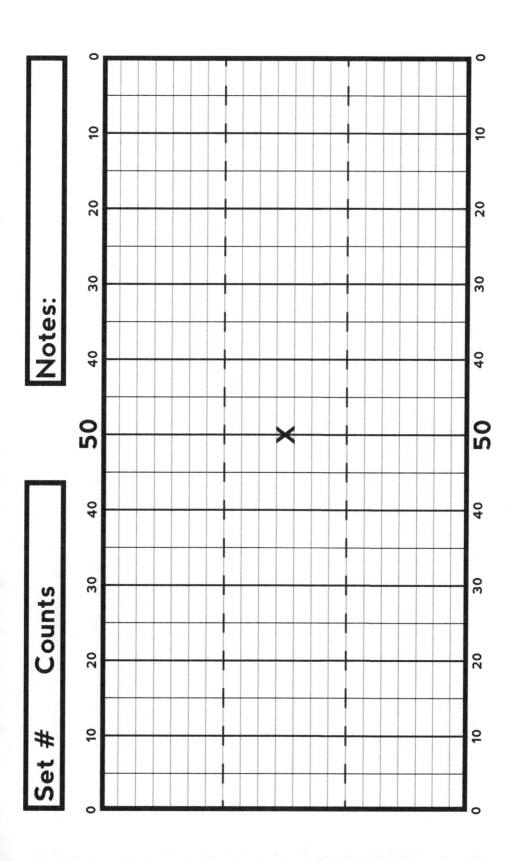

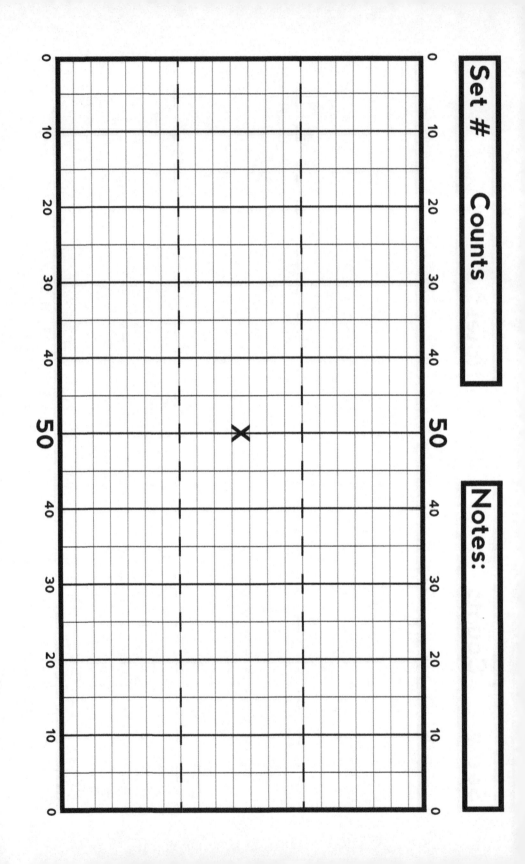

Set #   Counts

Notes:

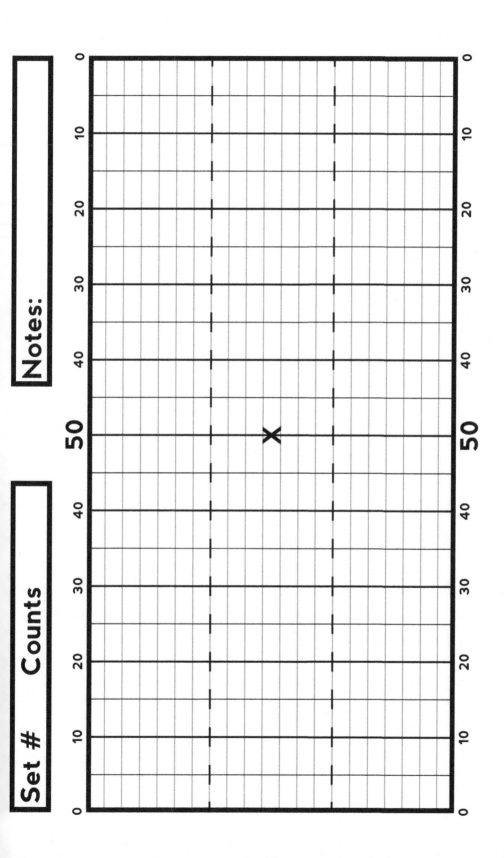

Notes:

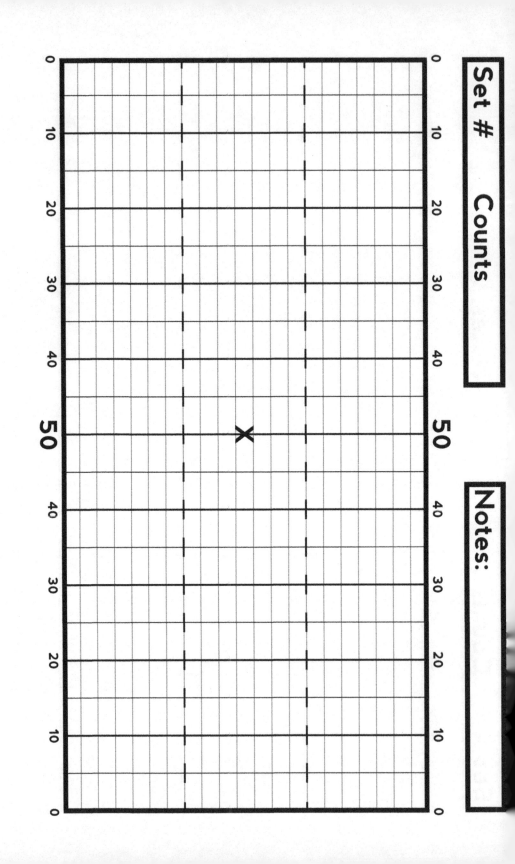

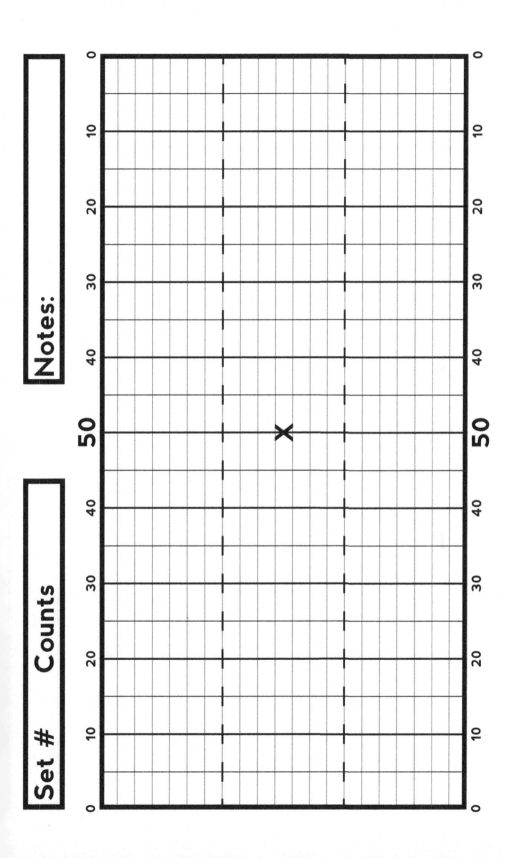

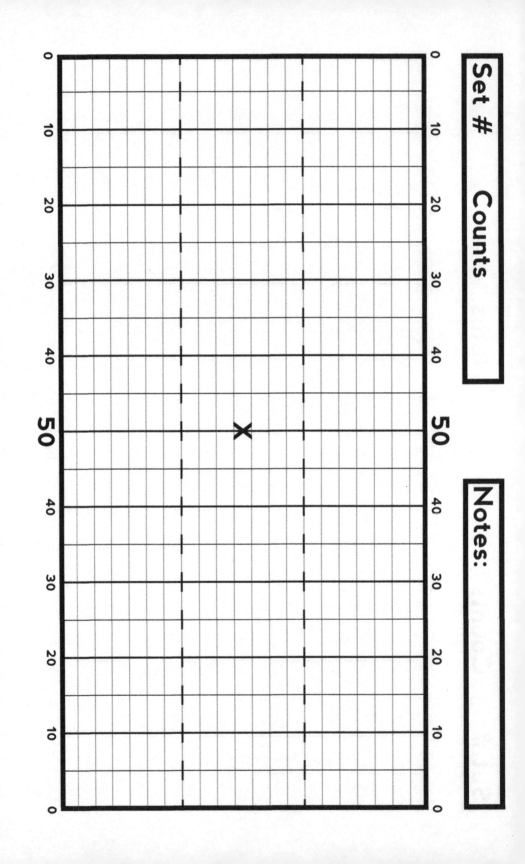

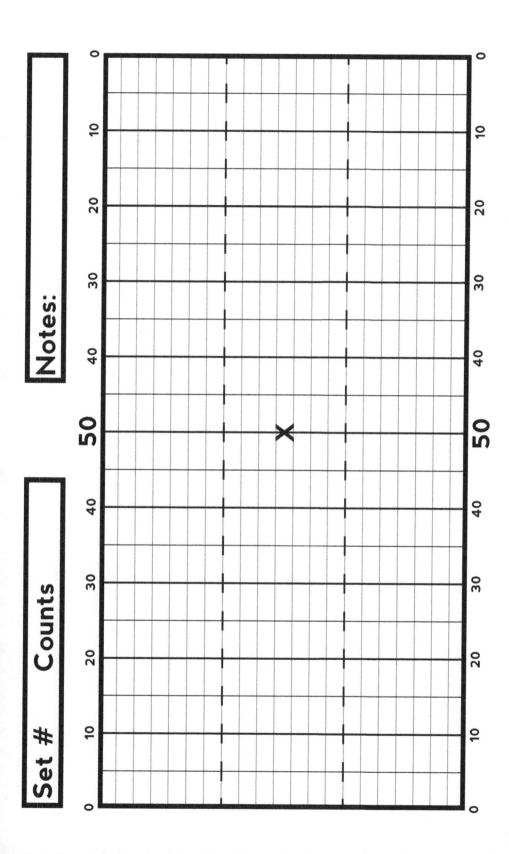

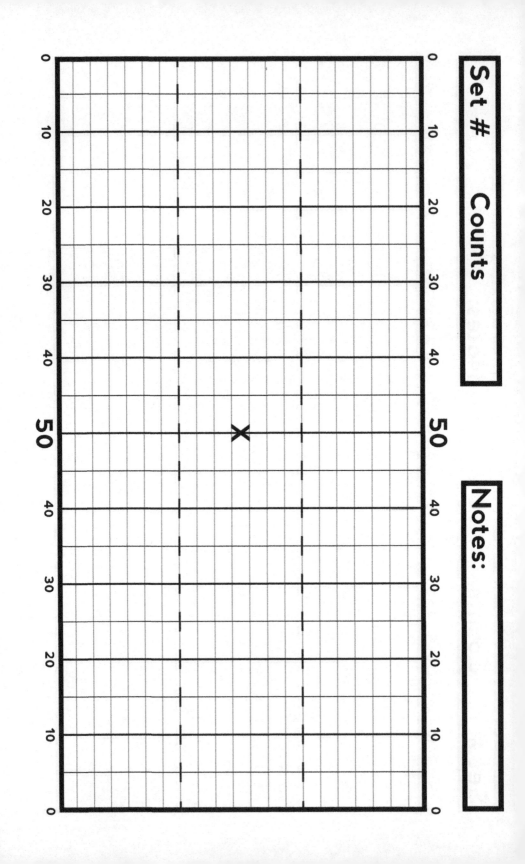

Set #   Counts   Notes:

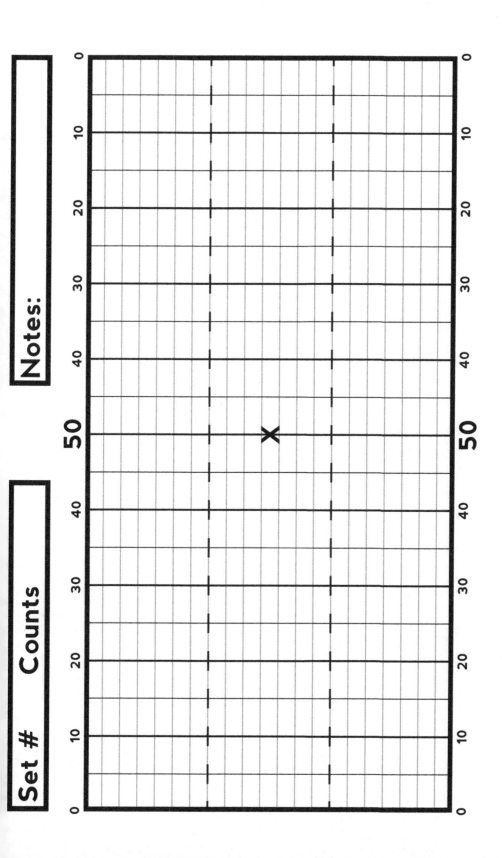

Set #   Counts

Notes:

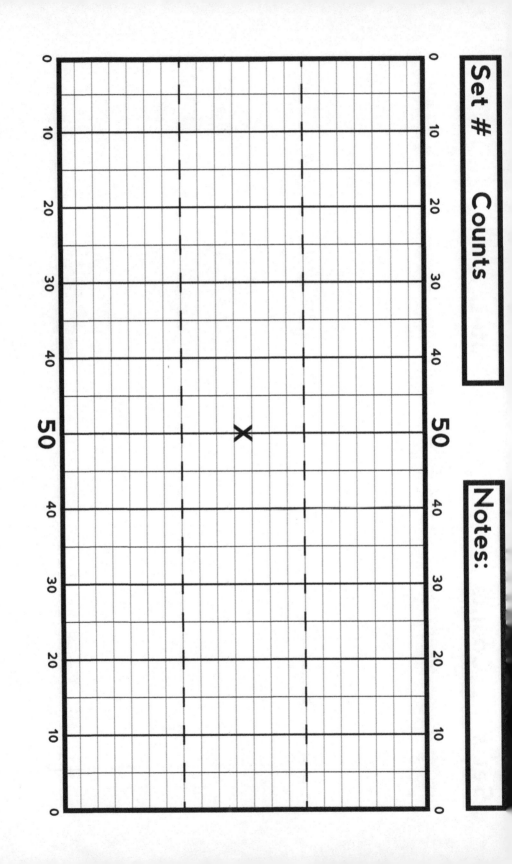

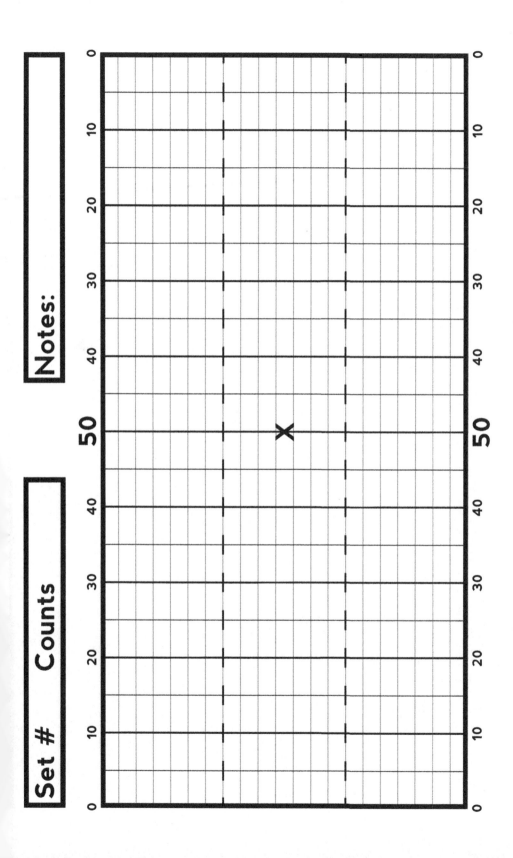

Set #　**Counts**　**Notes:**

Set #   Counts

Notes:

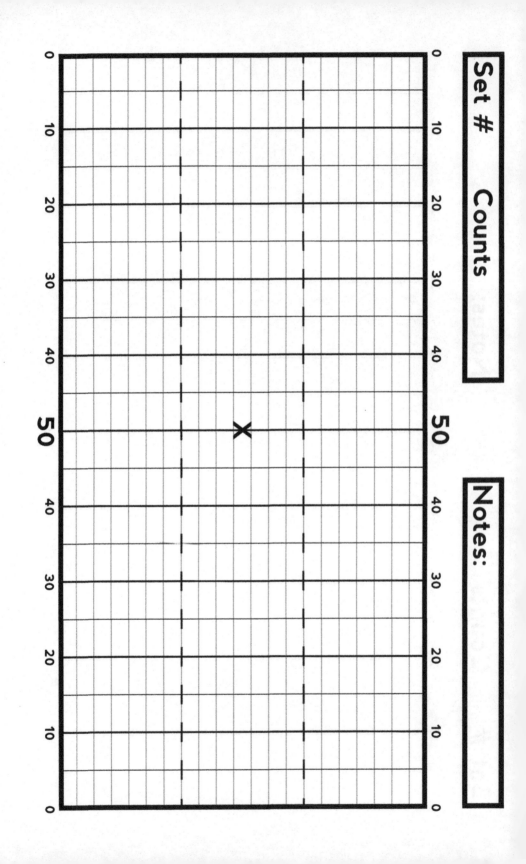

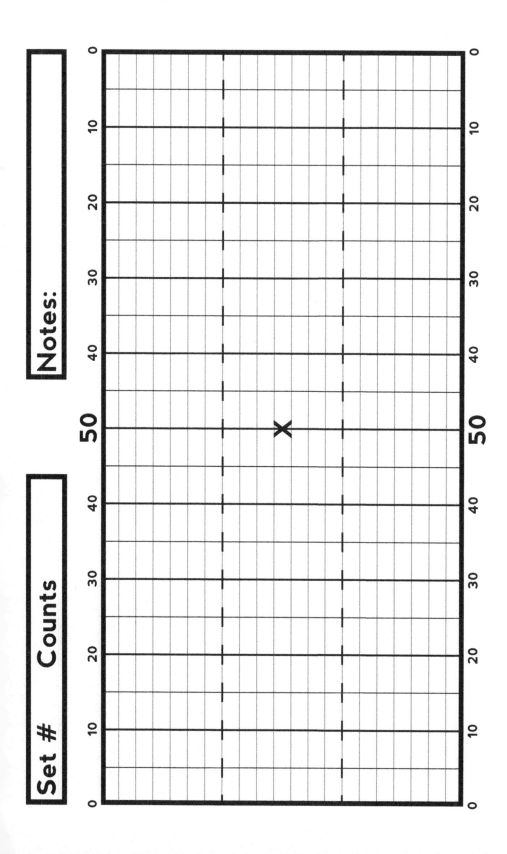

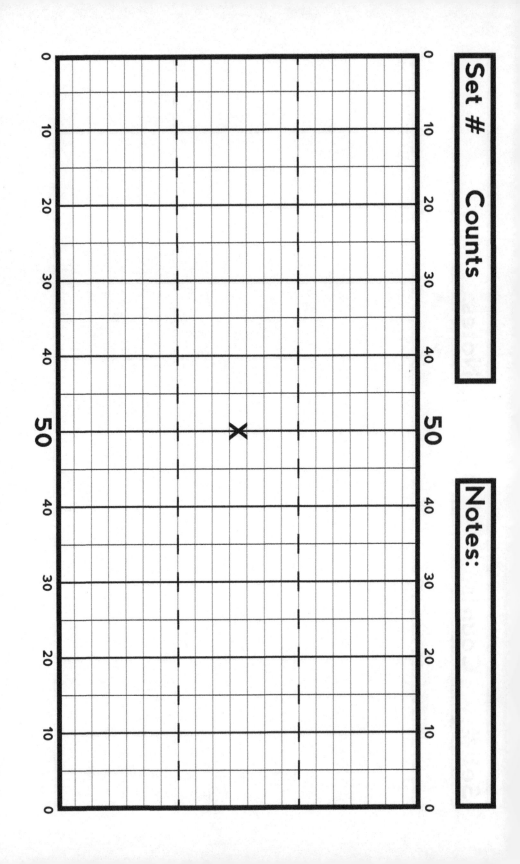

Set #　　Counts

Notes:

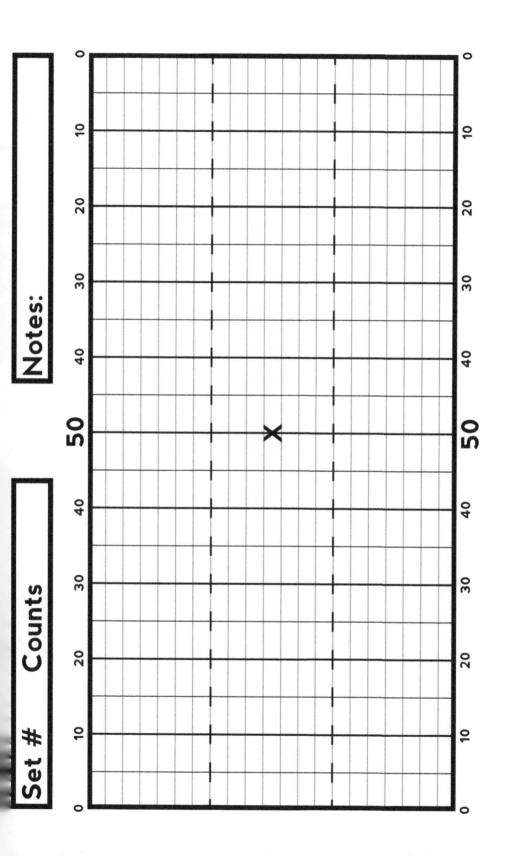

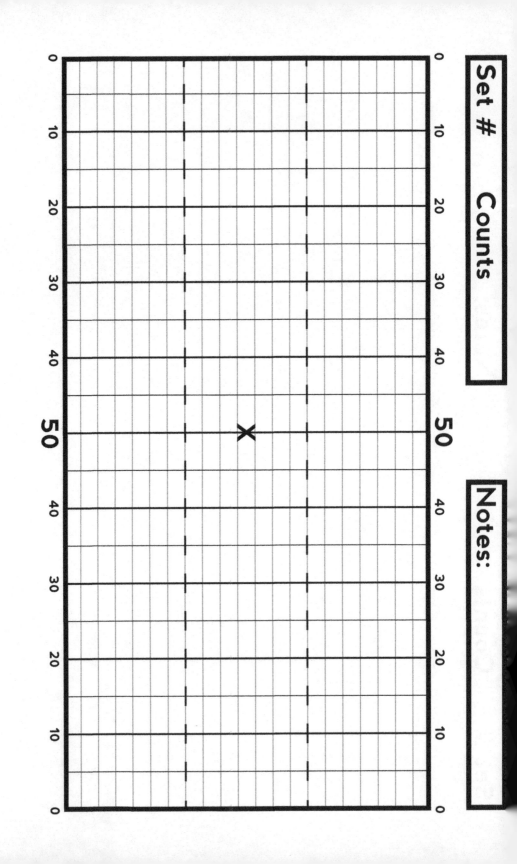

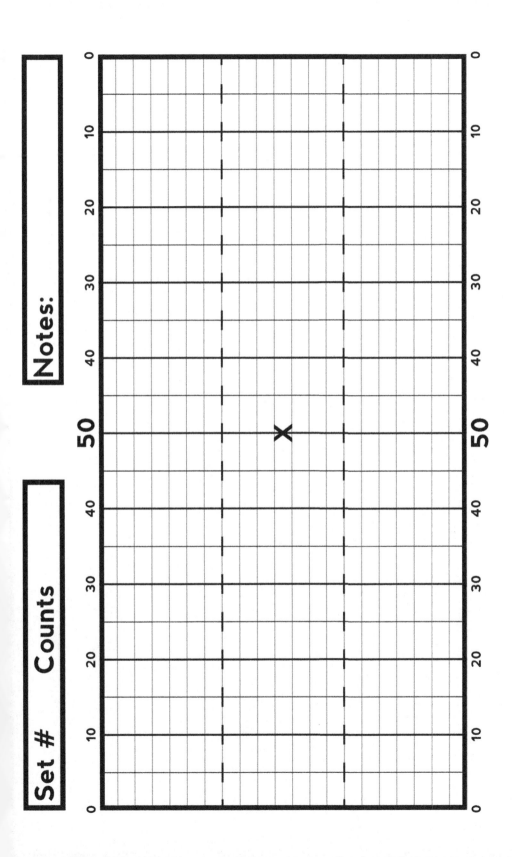

Notes:

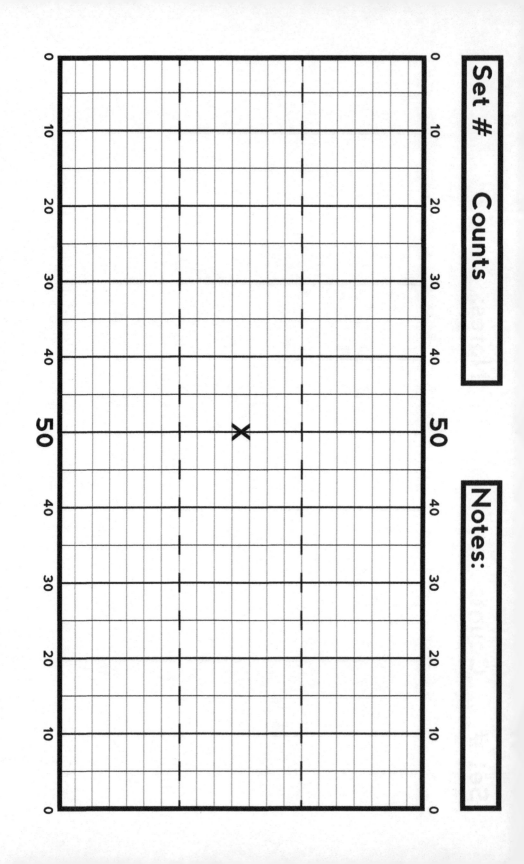

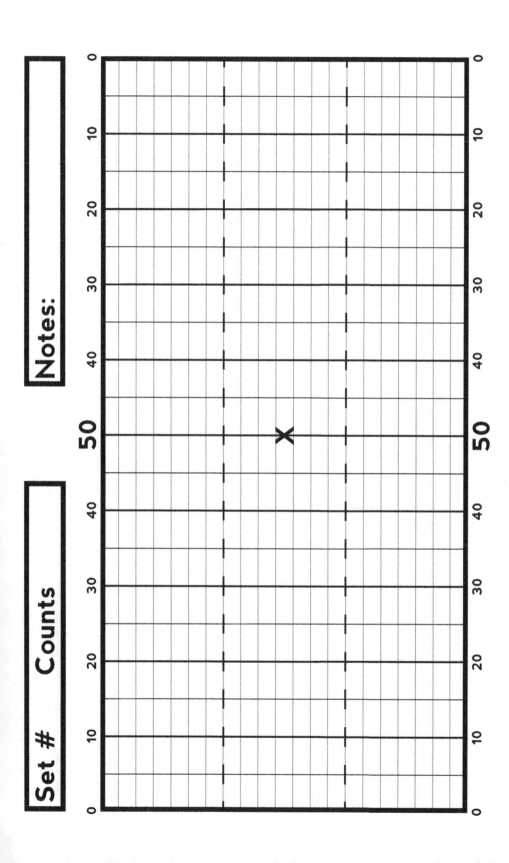

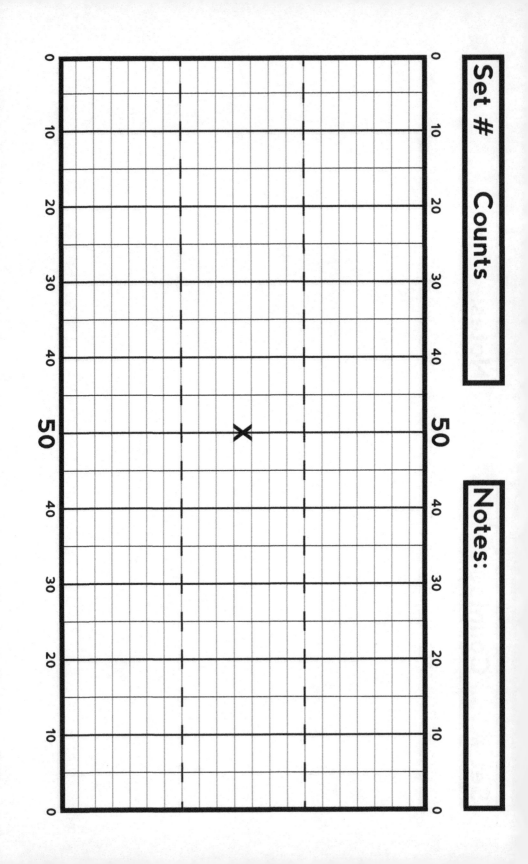

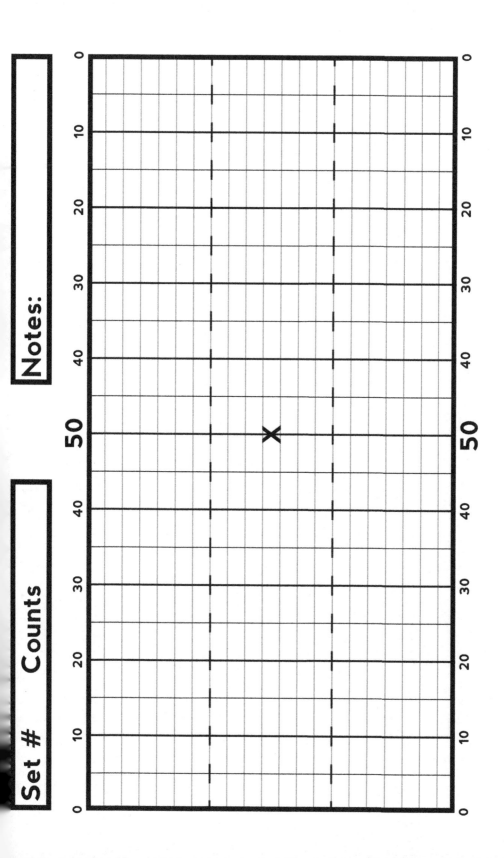

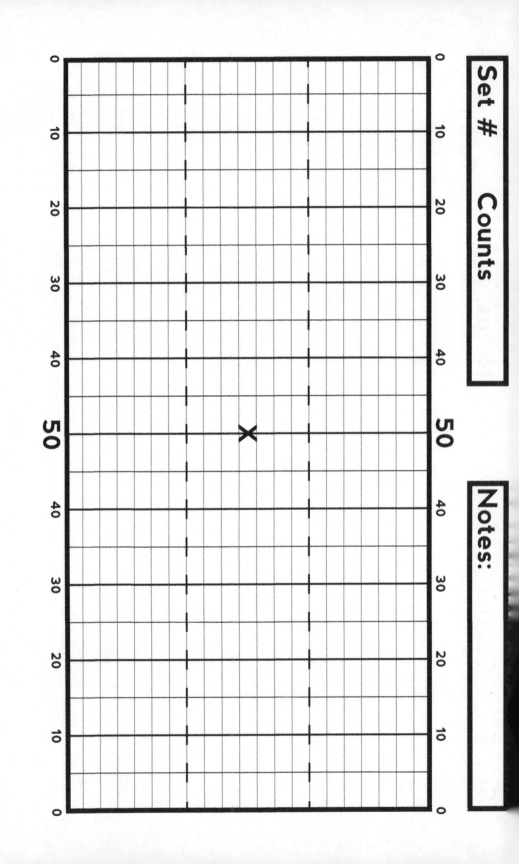

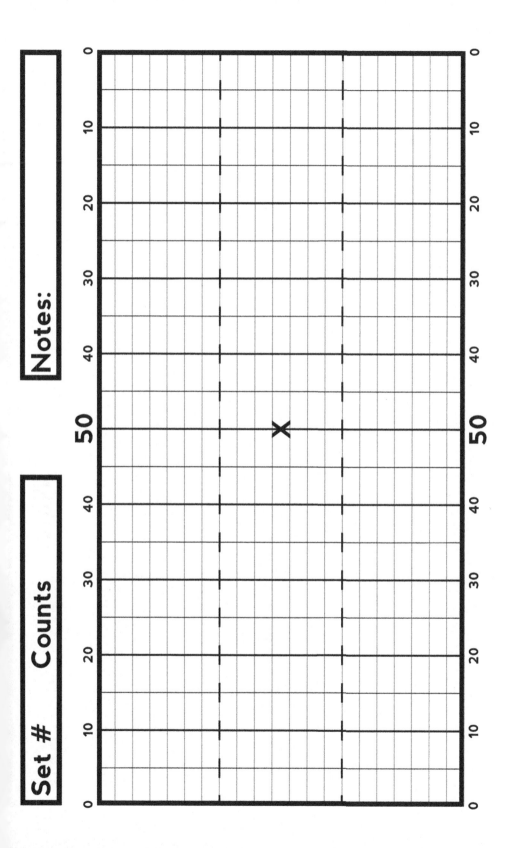

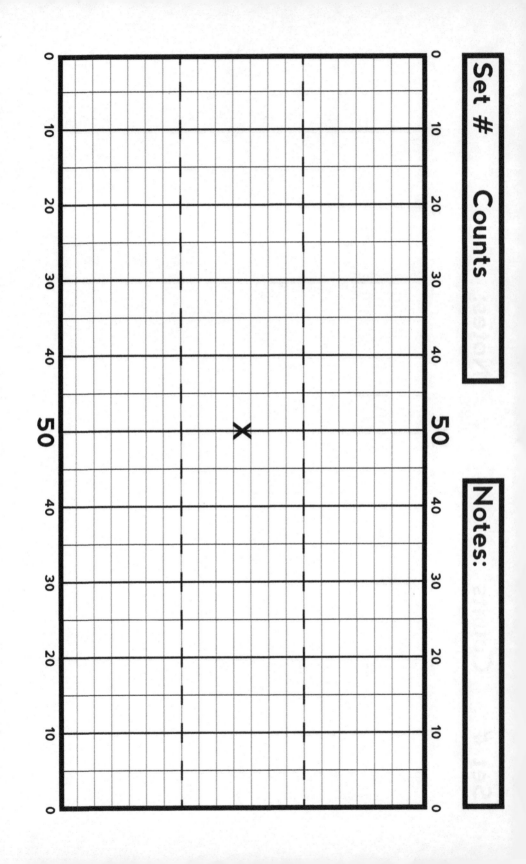

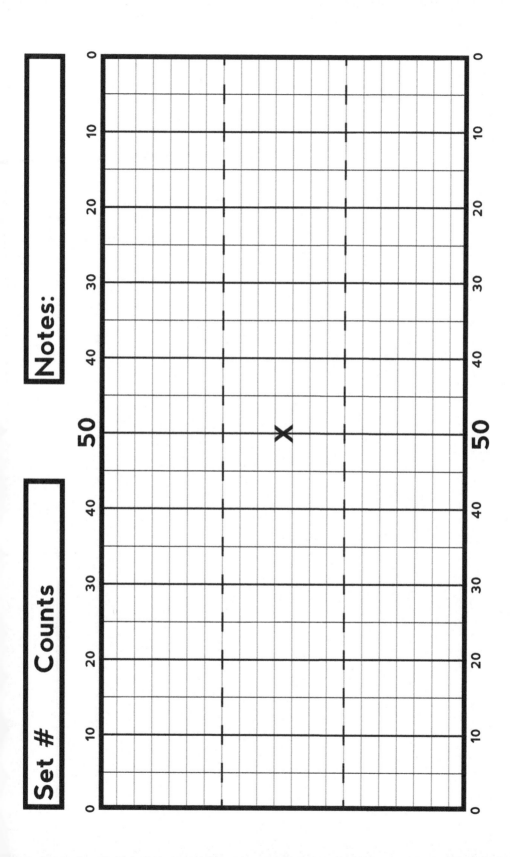

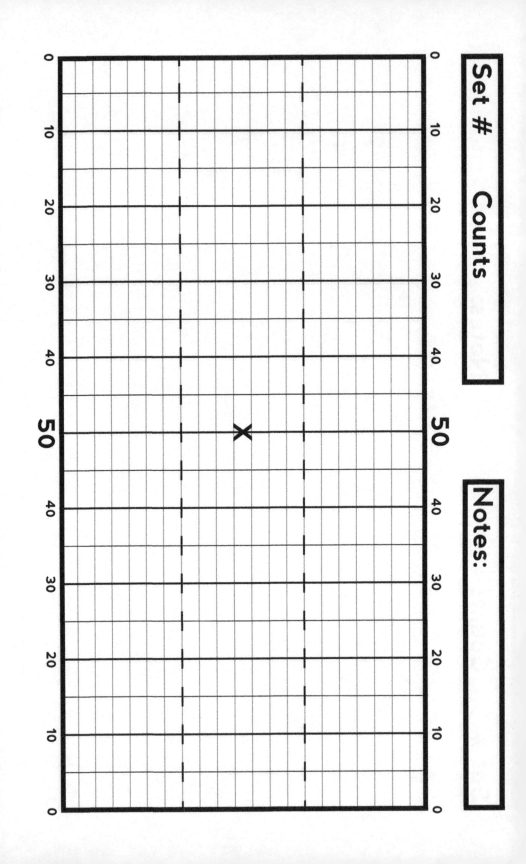

Set #   Counts

Notes:

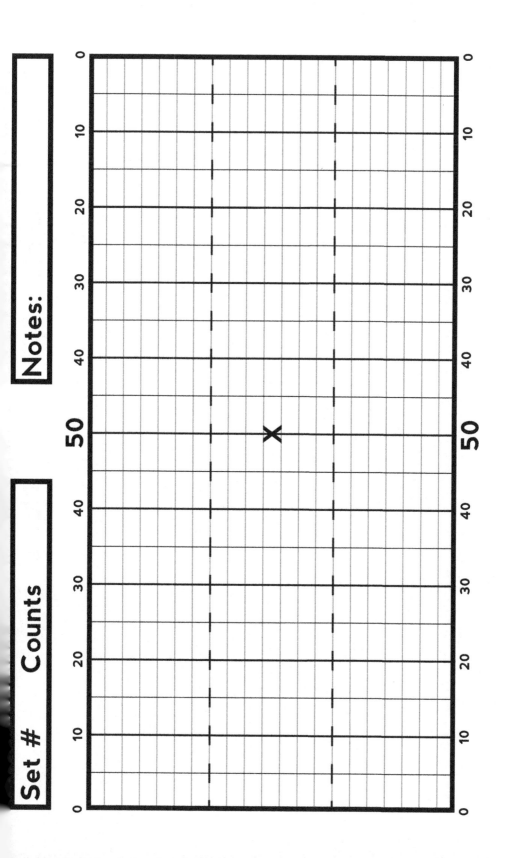

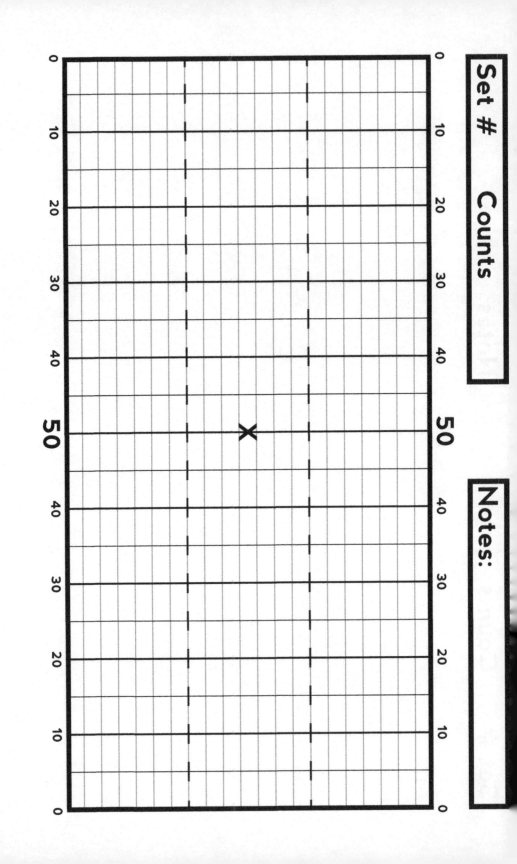

Set #   Counts

Notes:

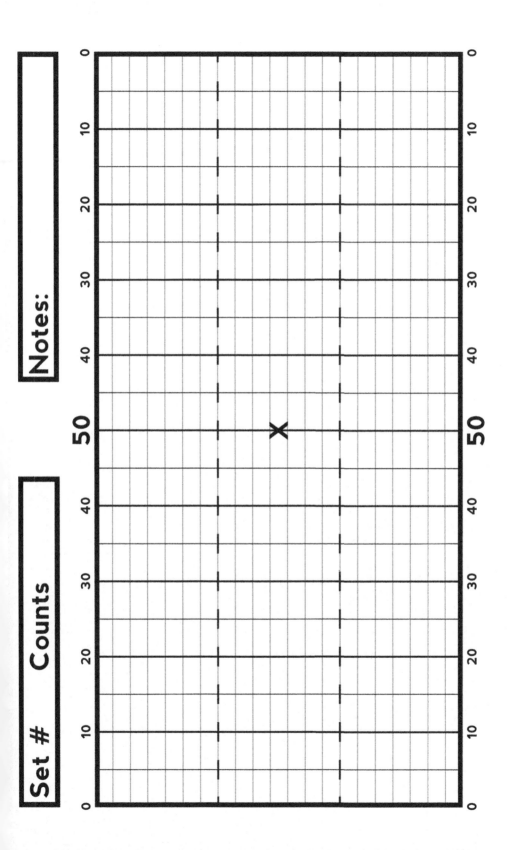

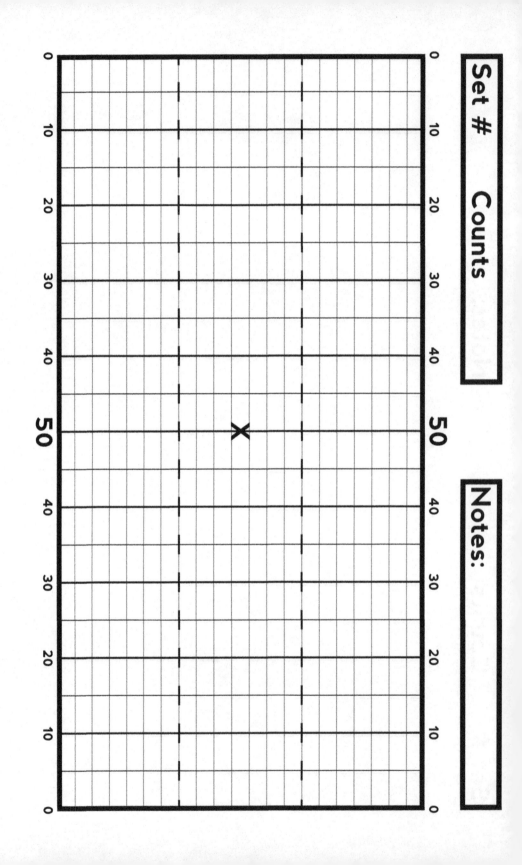

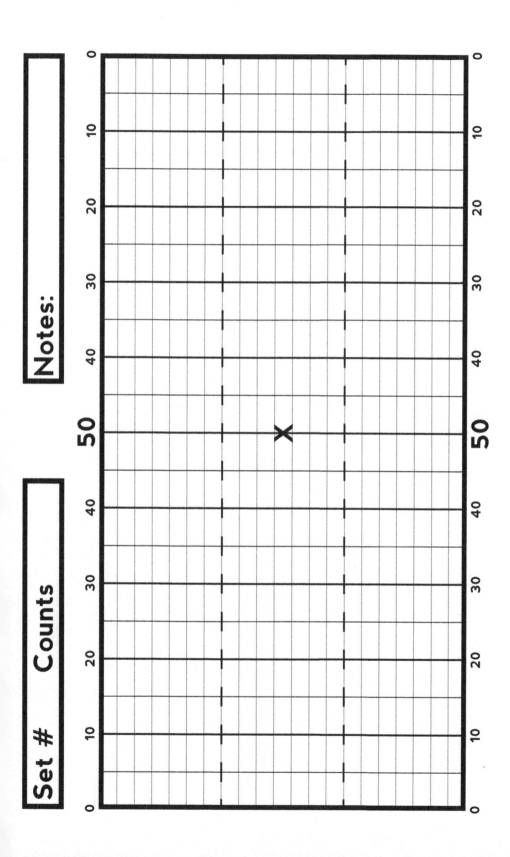

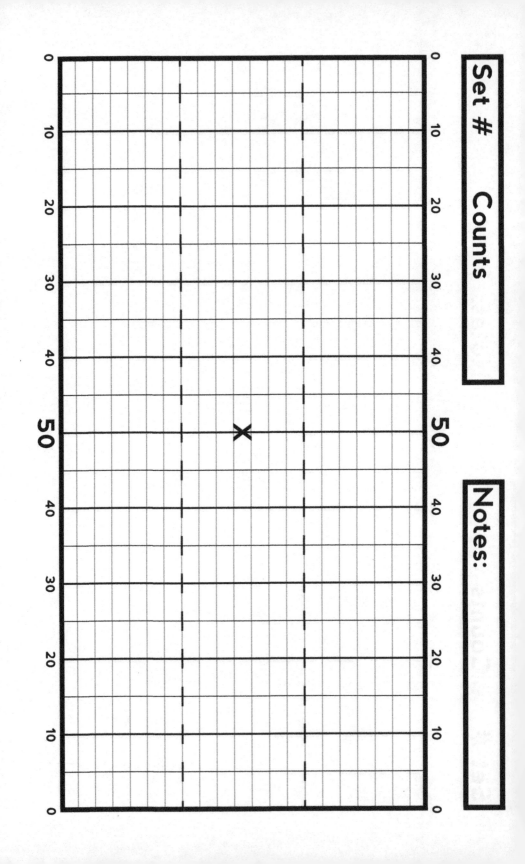

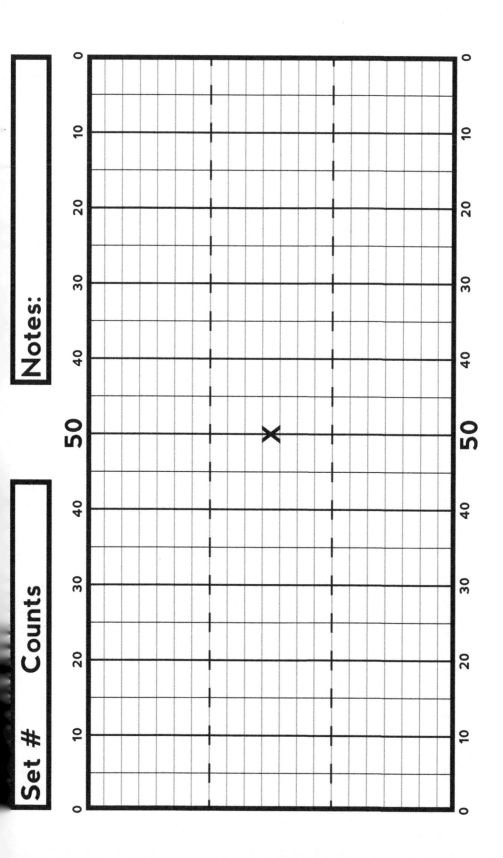

Counts

Notes:

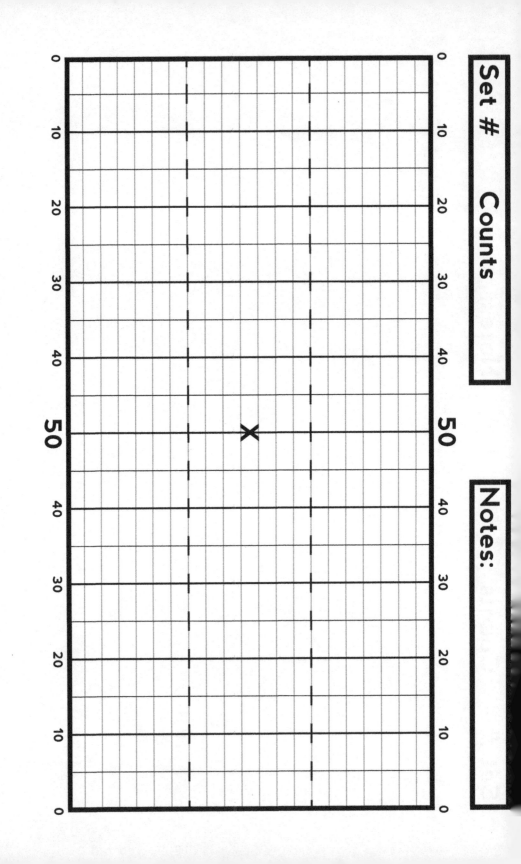

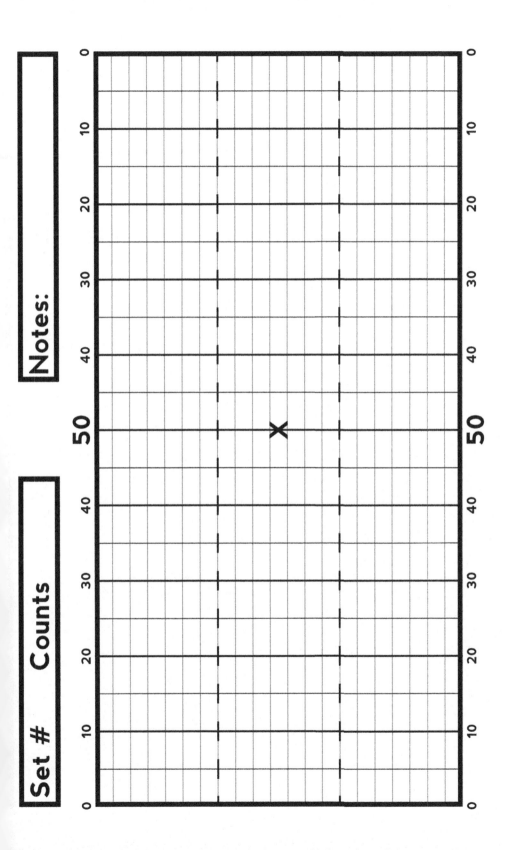

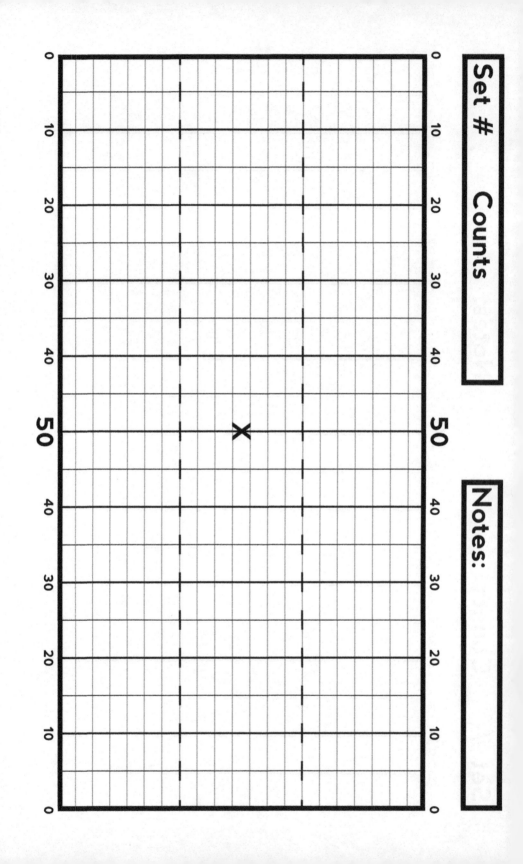

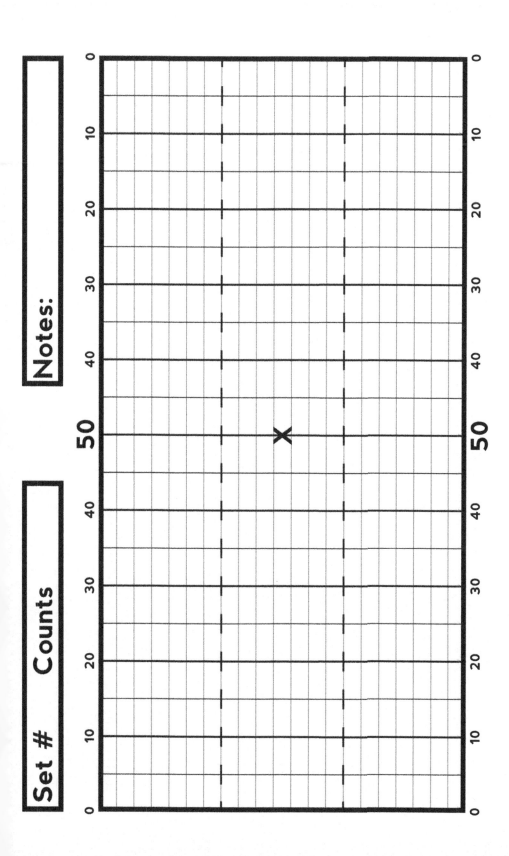

Notes:

Set #   Counts

Counts

Notes:

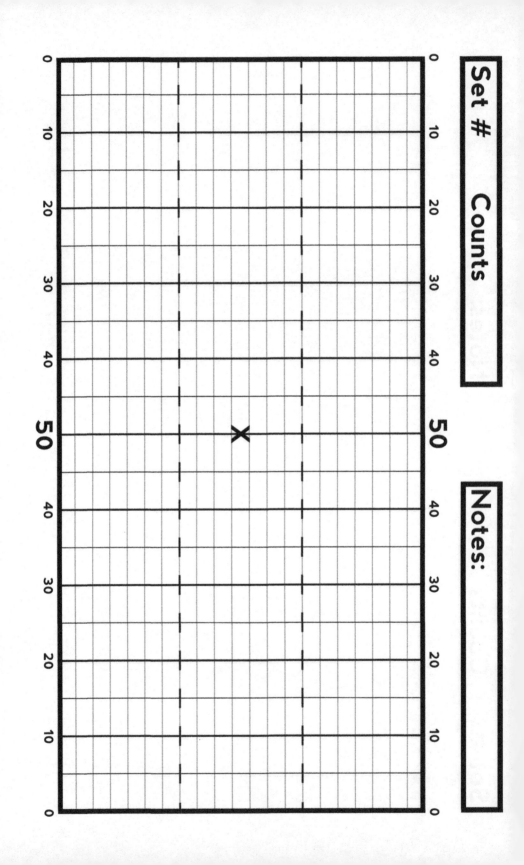

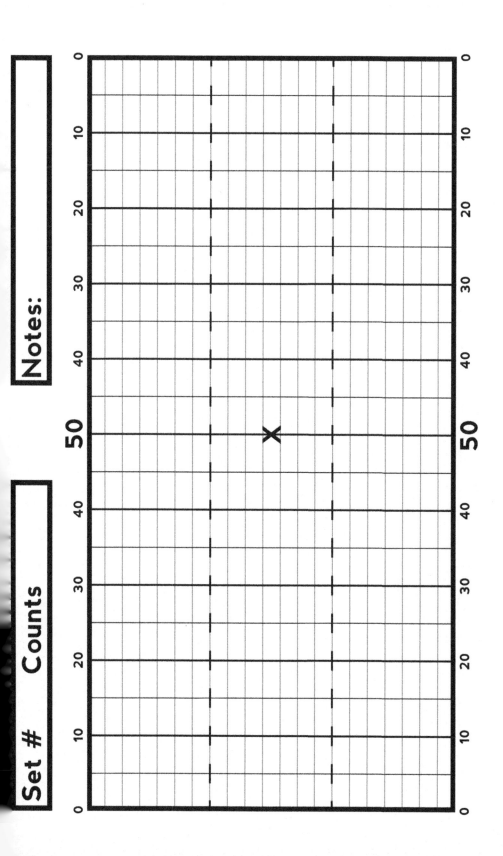

Counts

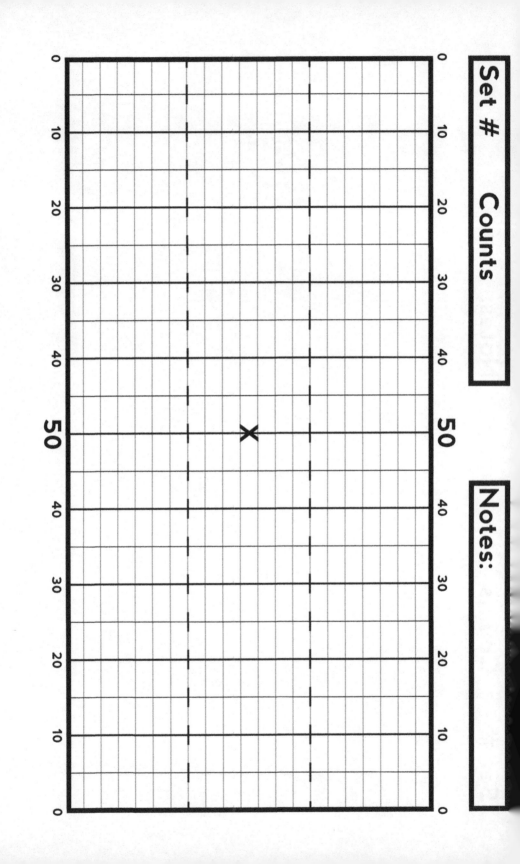

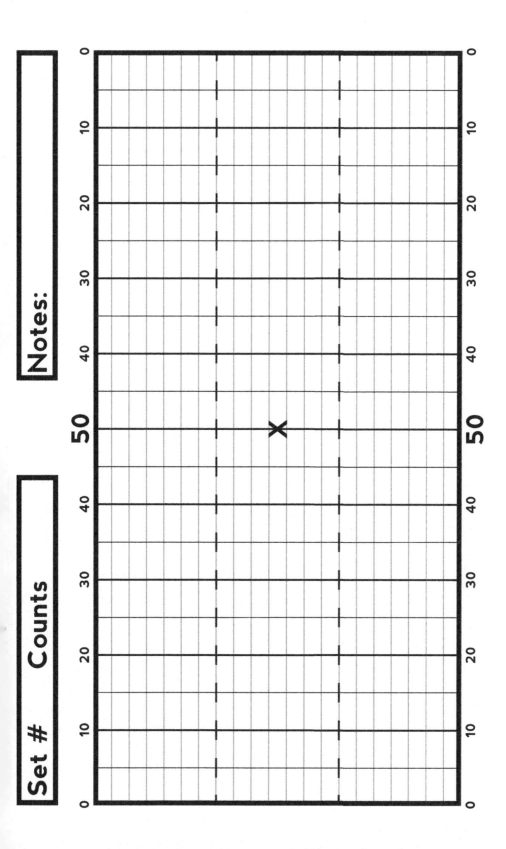

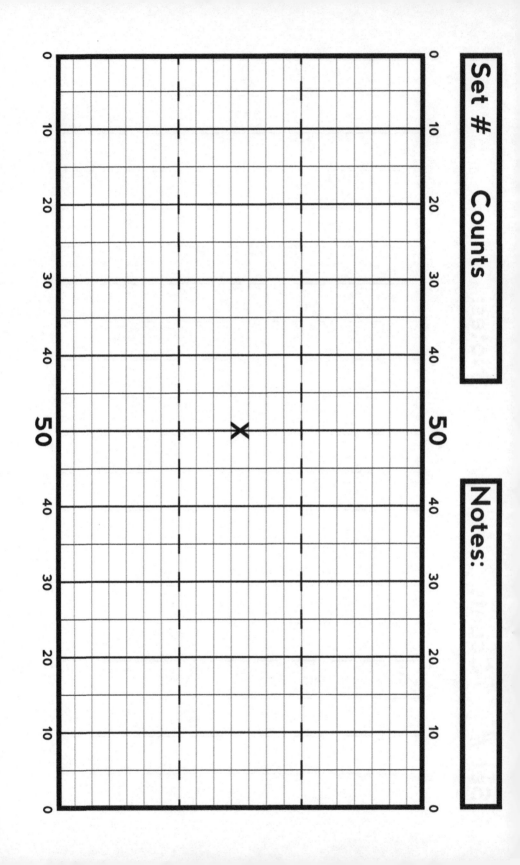

Set #   Counts

Notes:

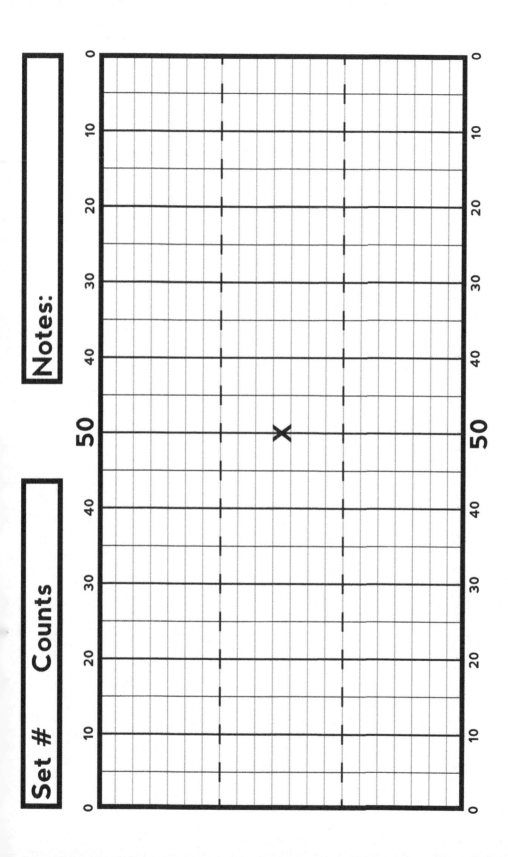

Set #   Counts

Counts

Notes:

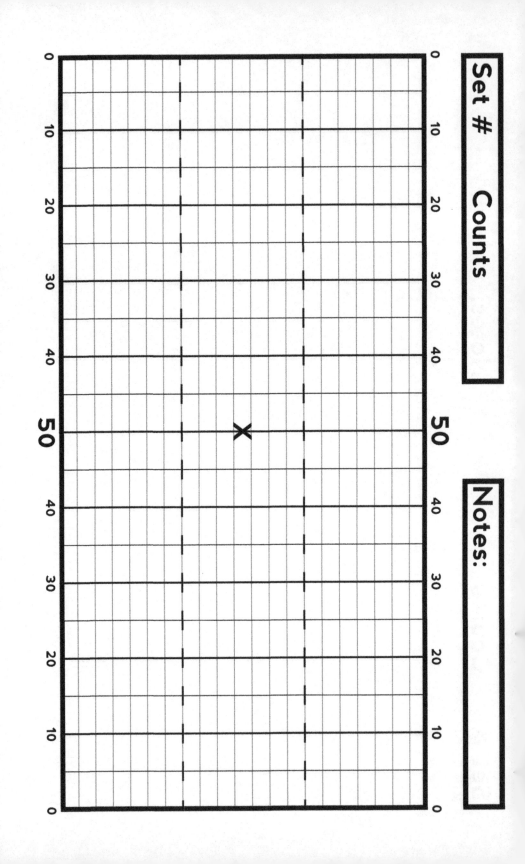

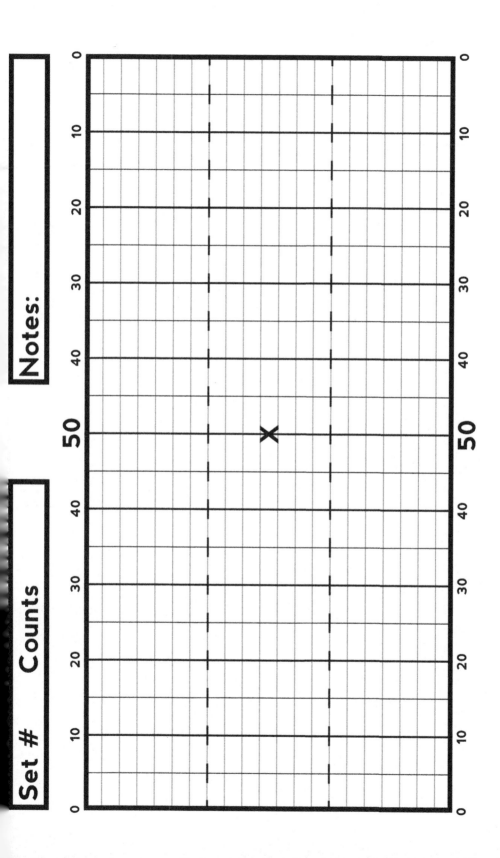

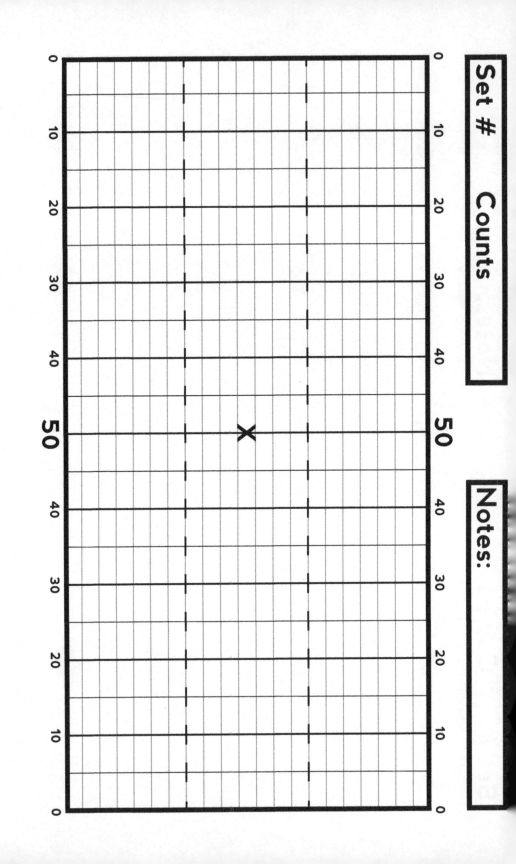

Set #   Counts

Notes:

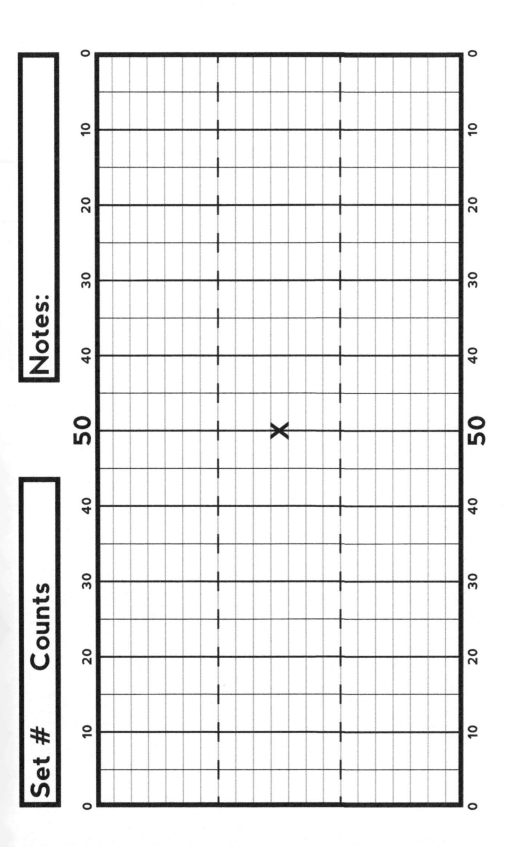

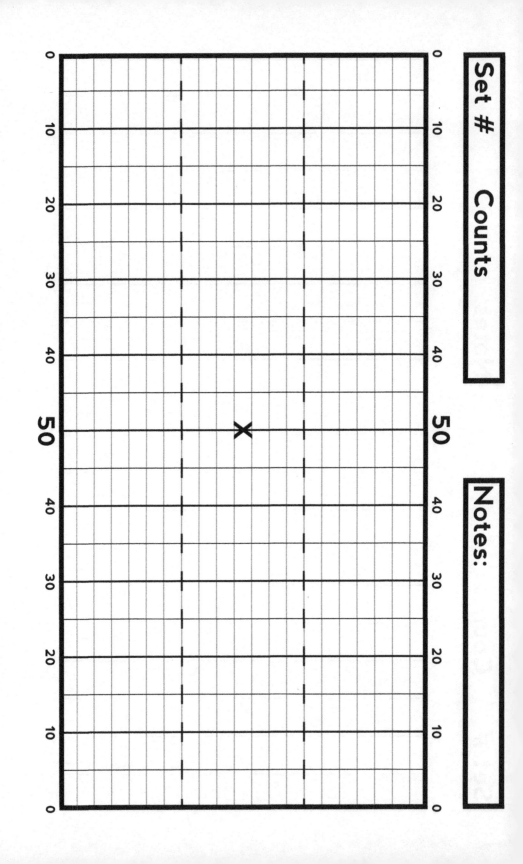

Set #   Counts

Notes:

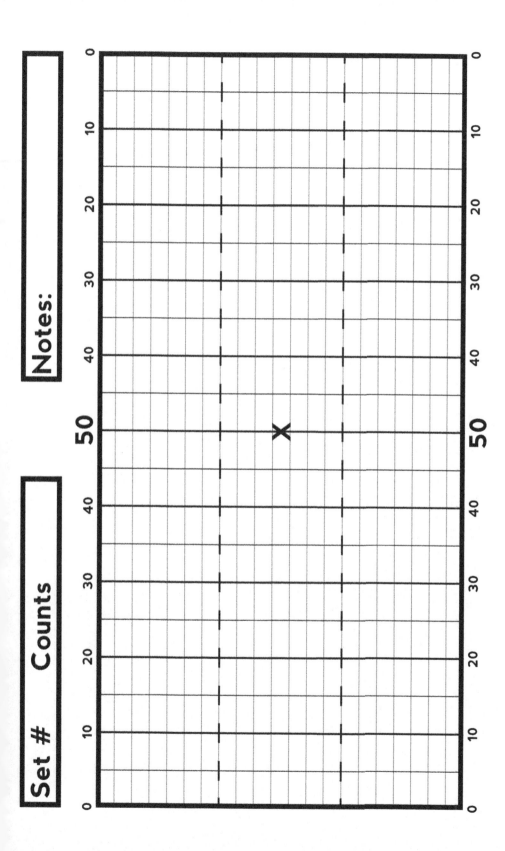

Notes:

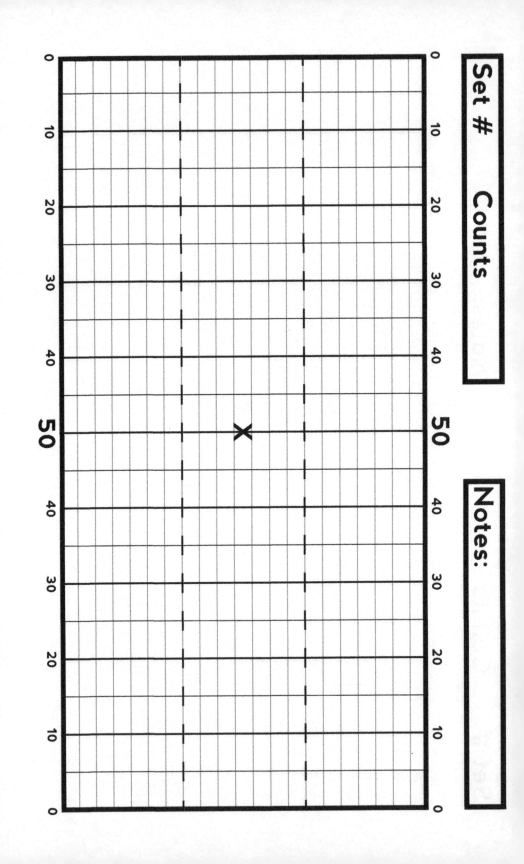

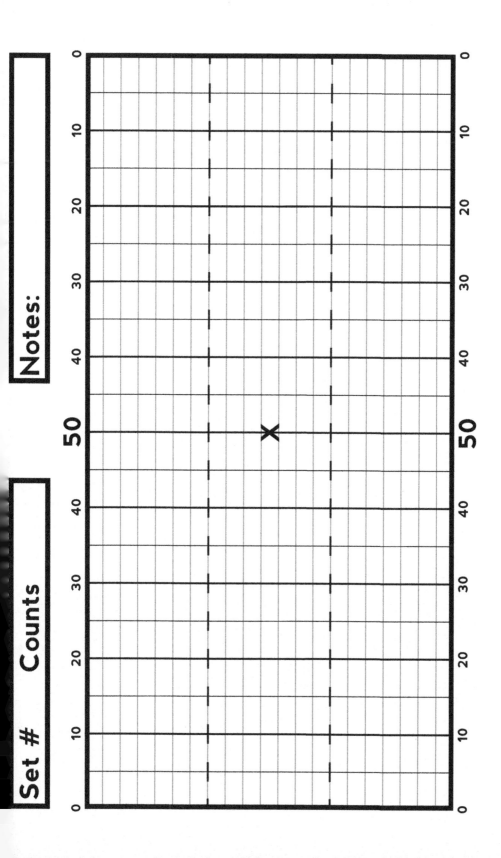

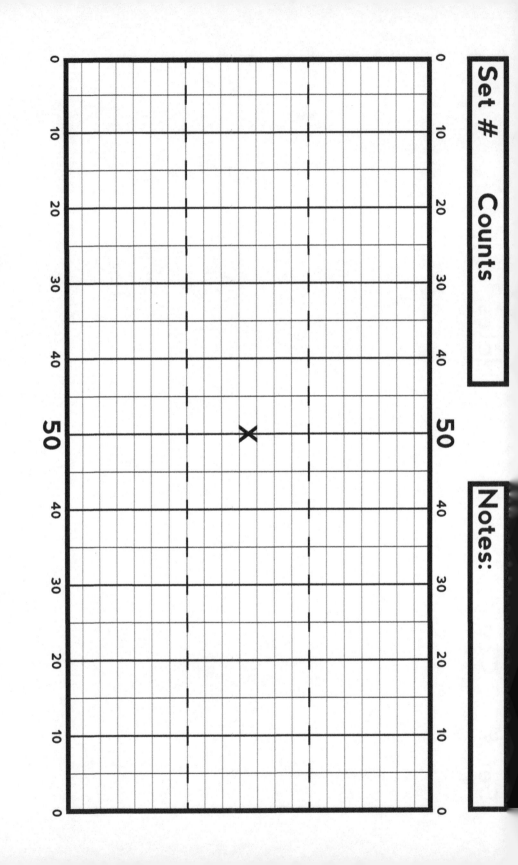

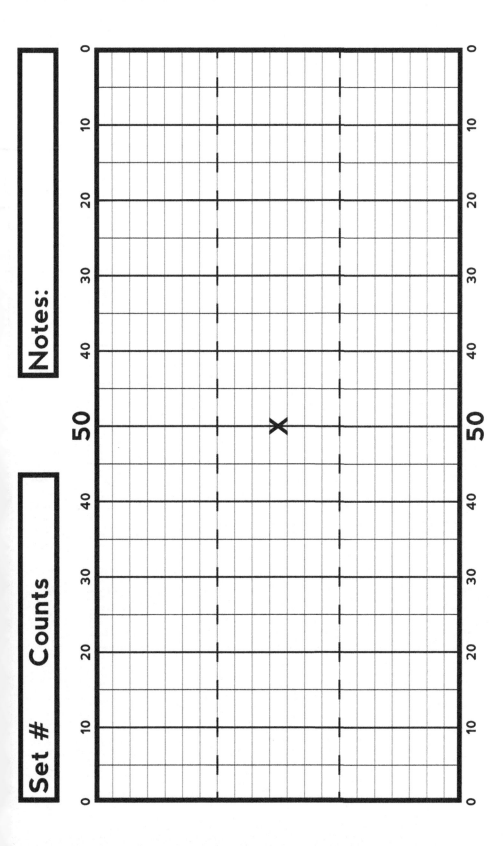

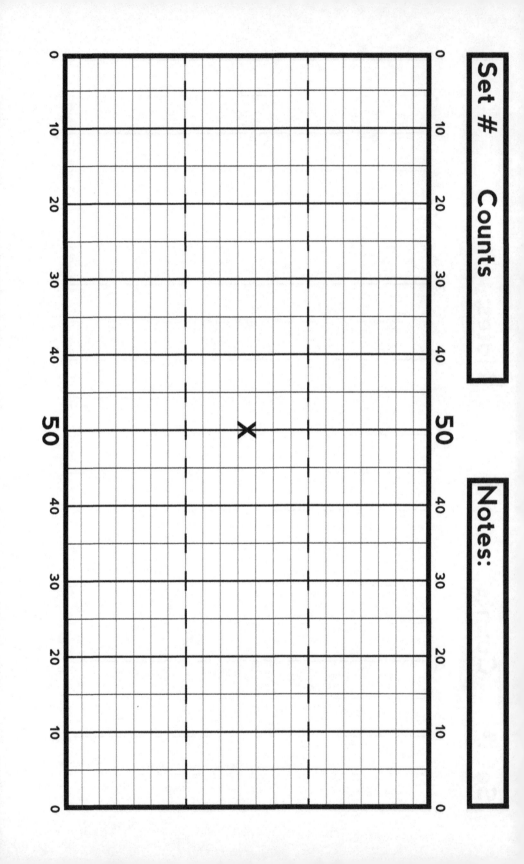

Set # Counts

Notes:

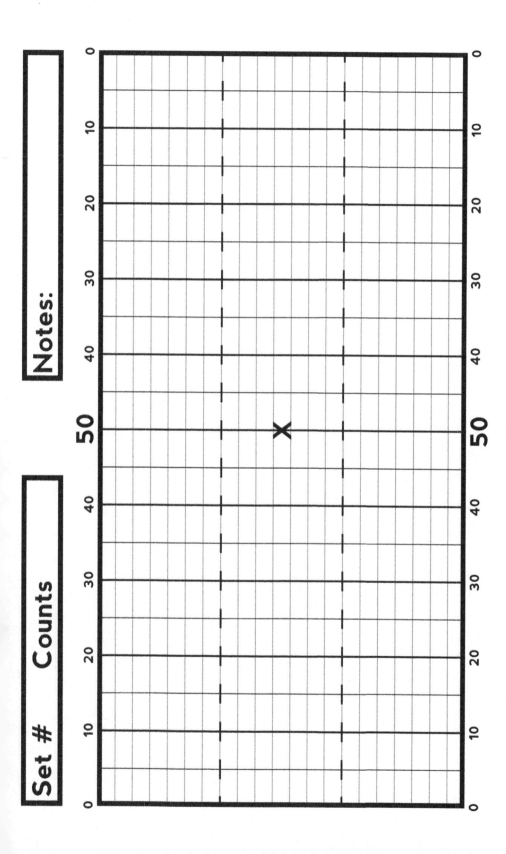

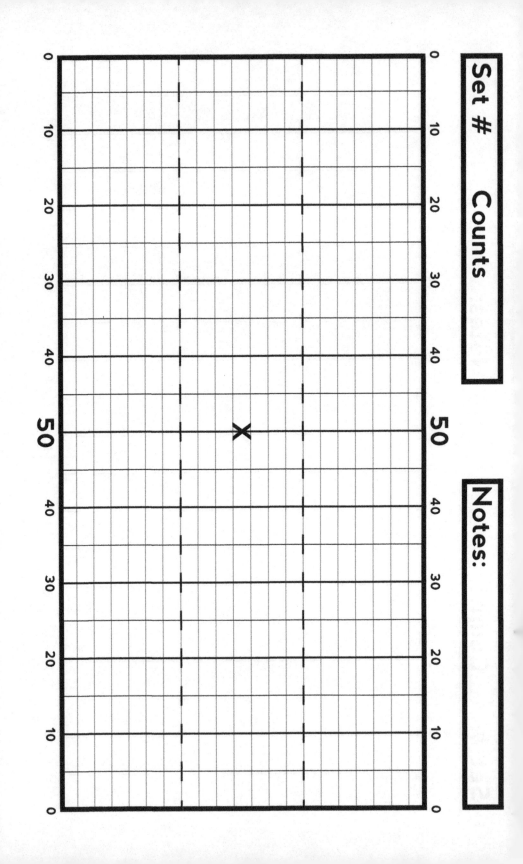

Set #   Counts

Notes:

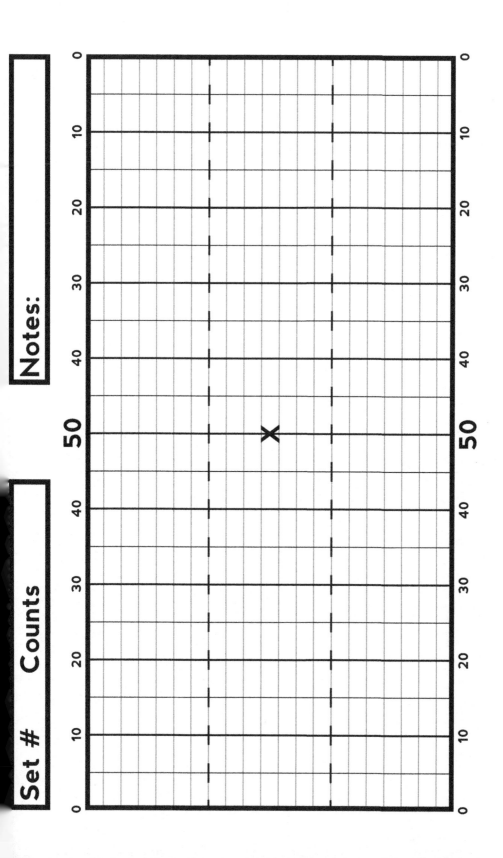

Set #   Counts

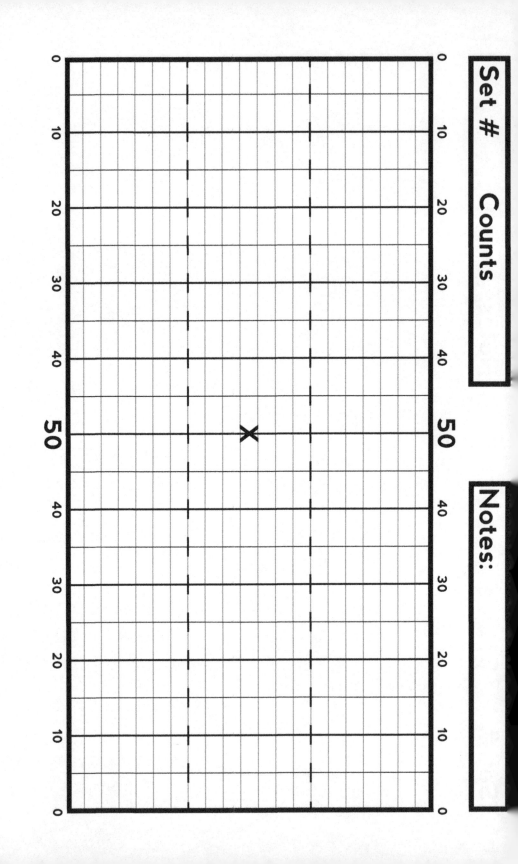

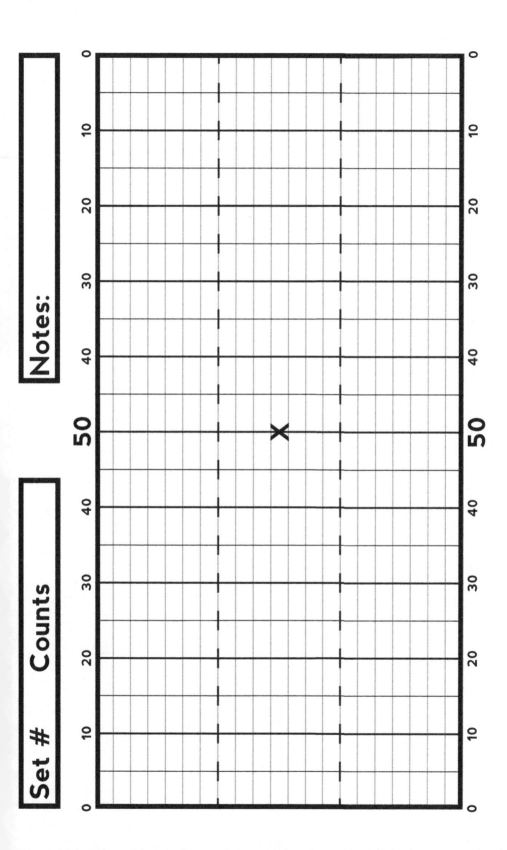

Notes:

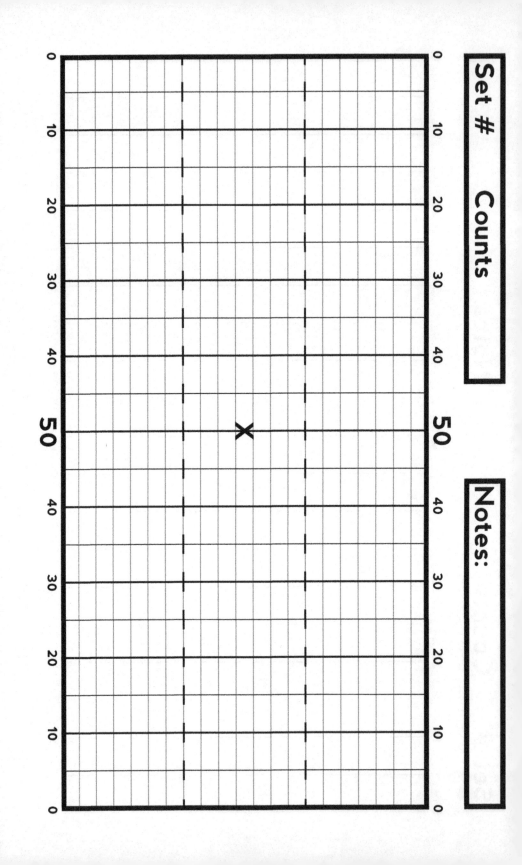

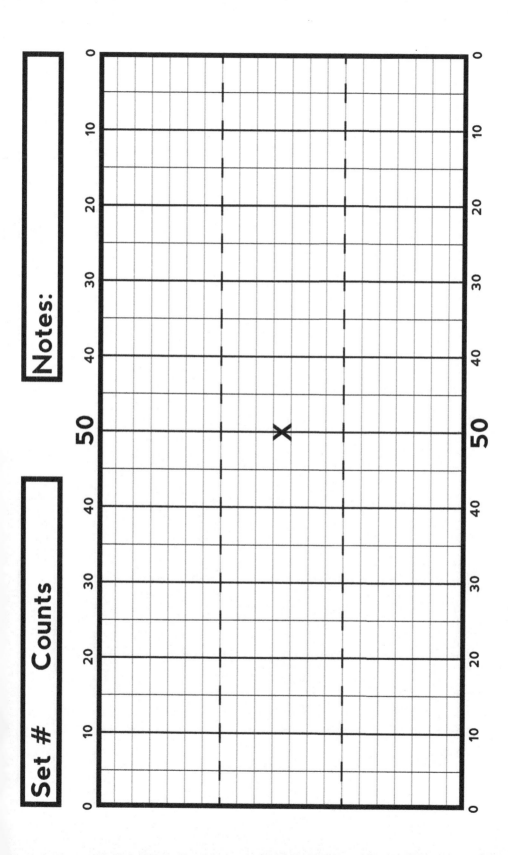

Notes:

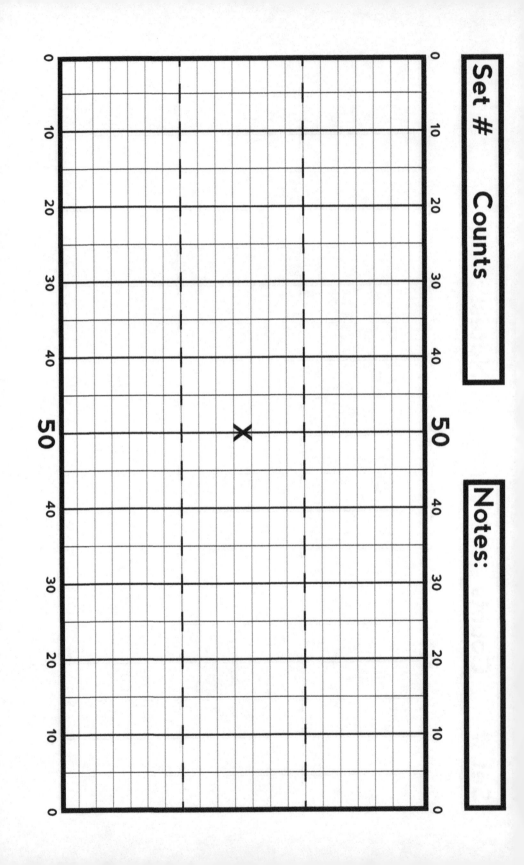

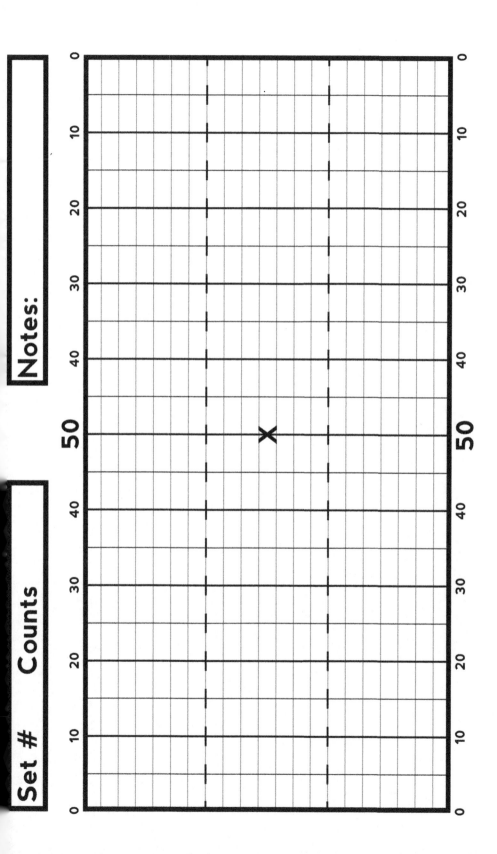

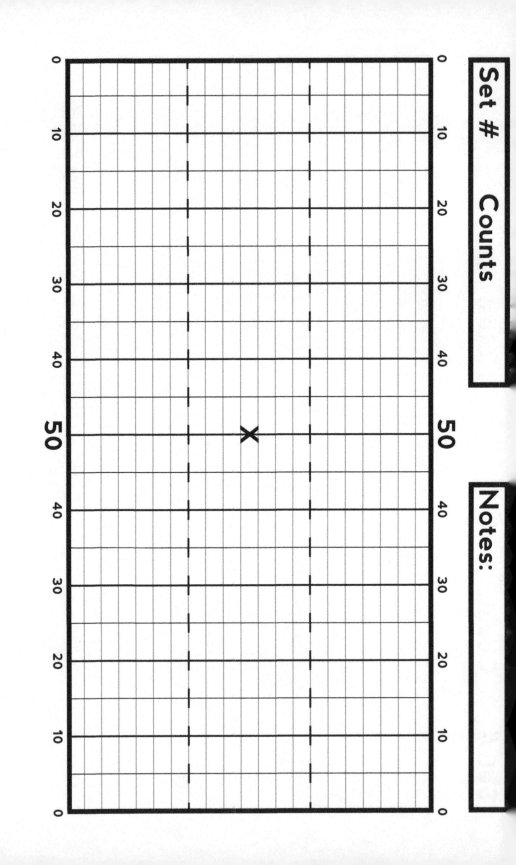

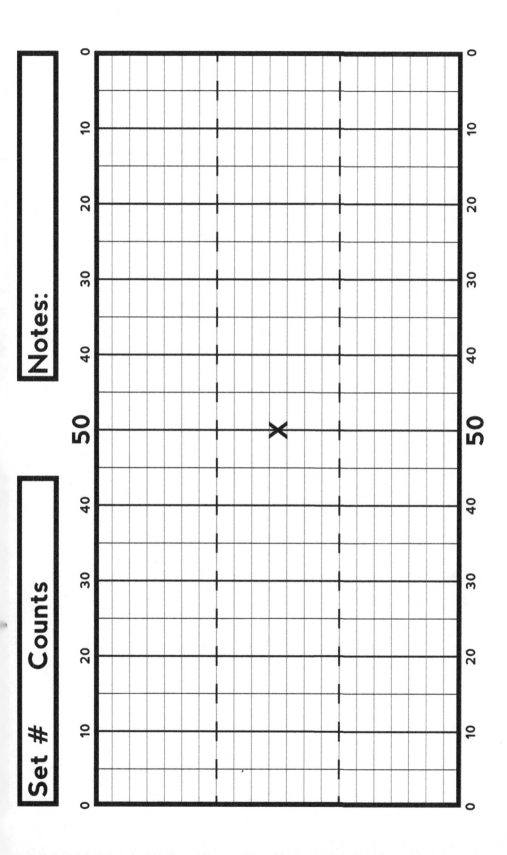

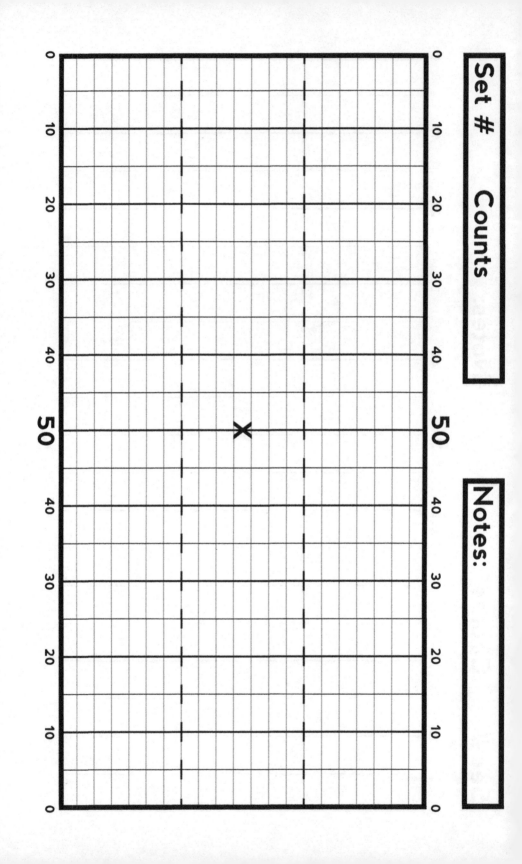

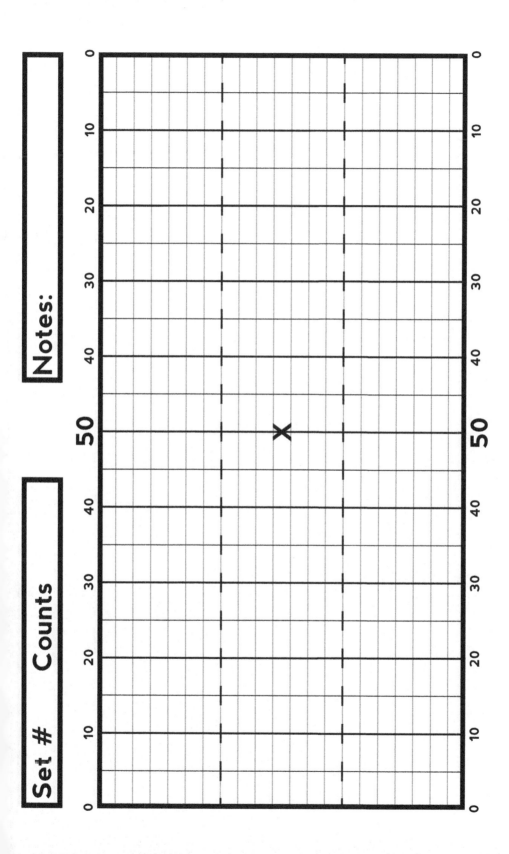

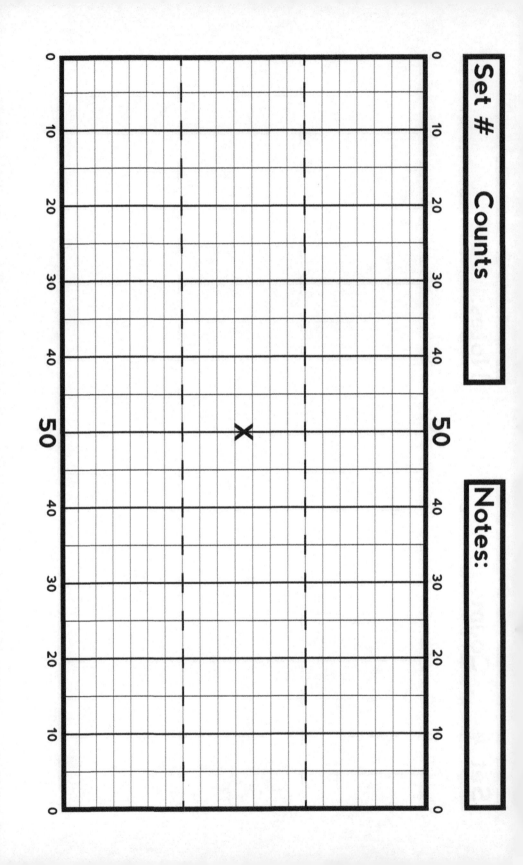

Set #   Counts

Notes:

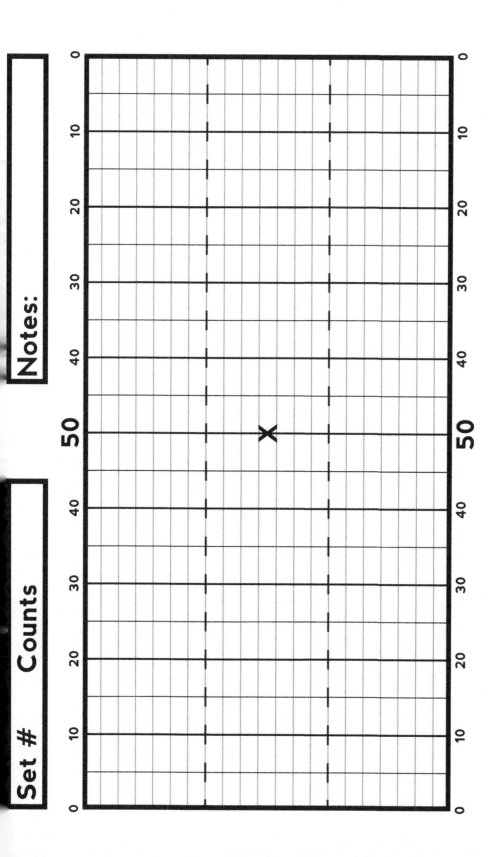

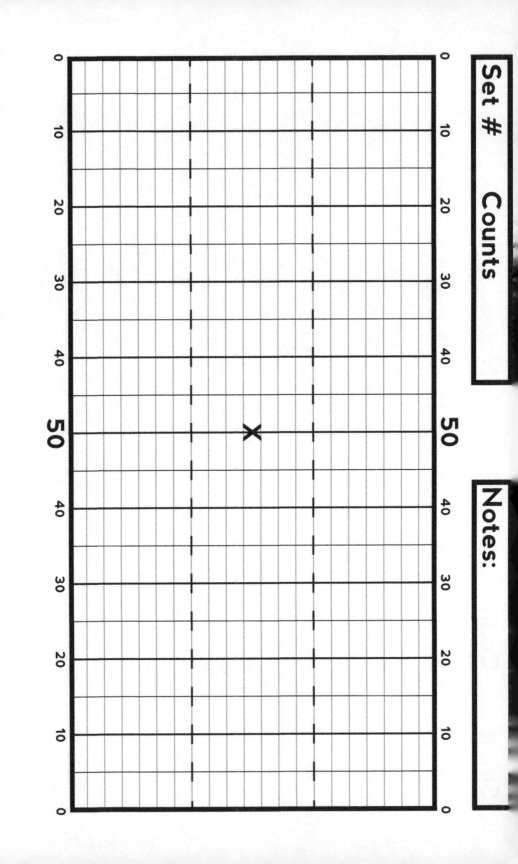

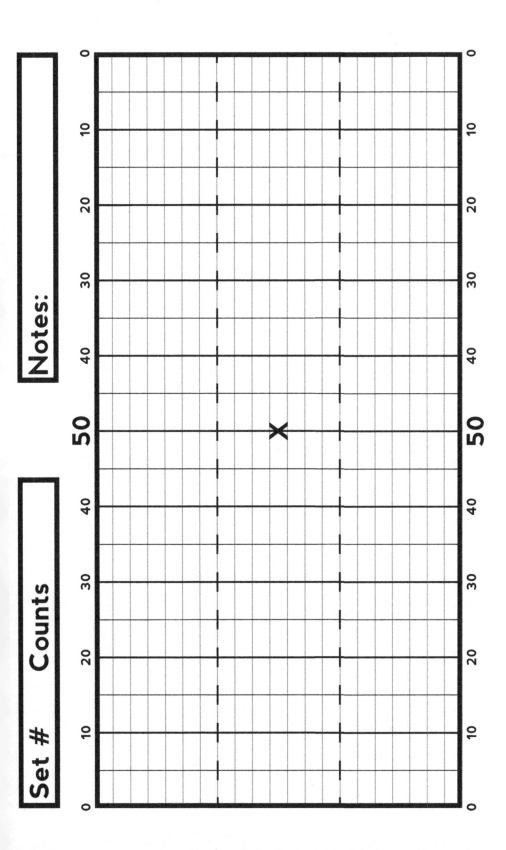

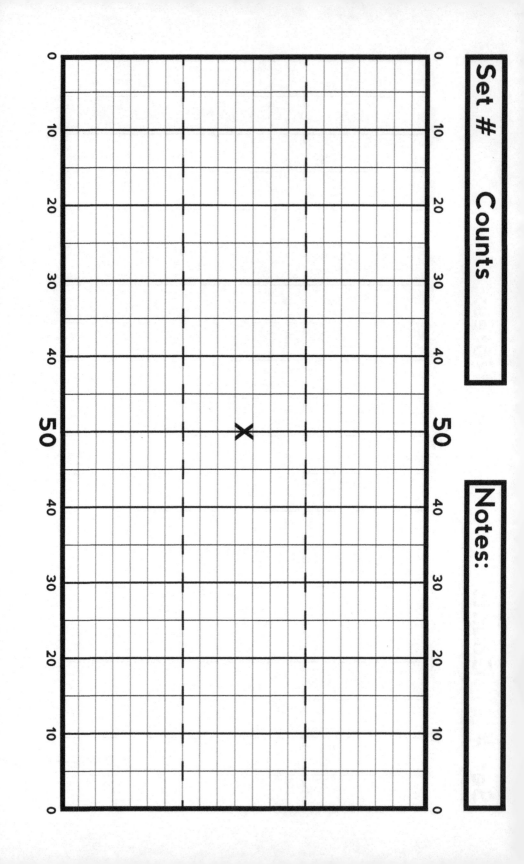

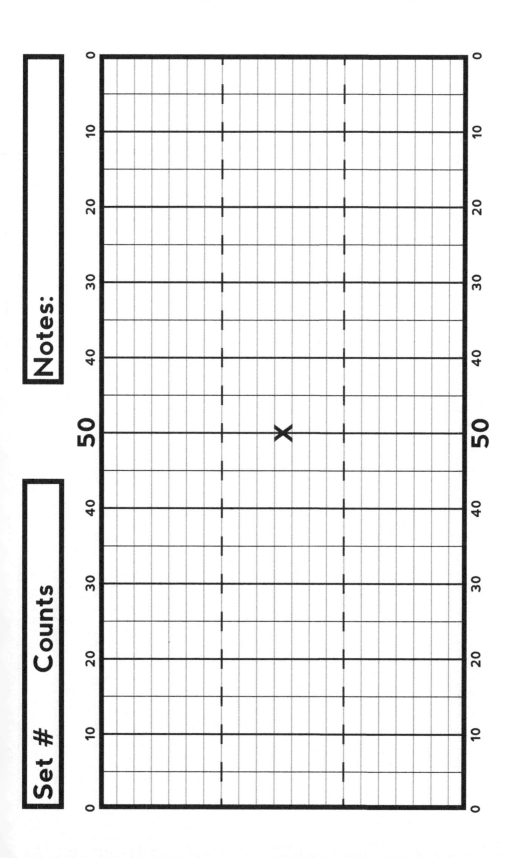

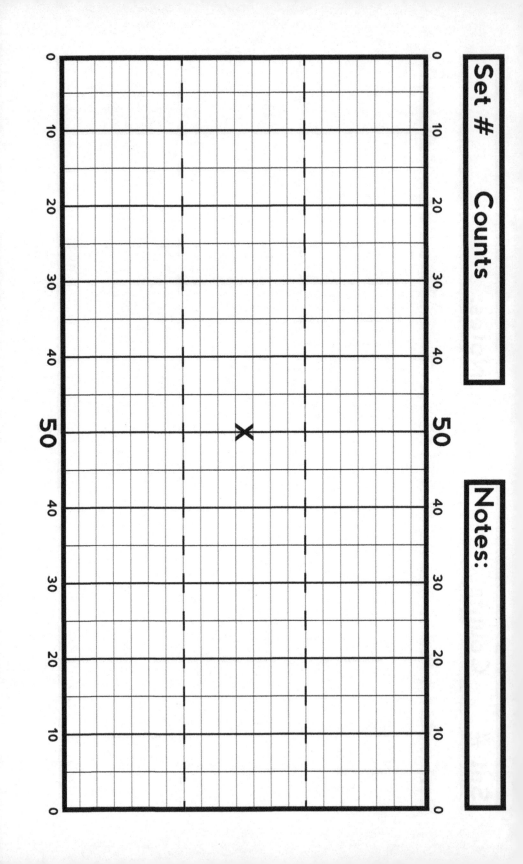

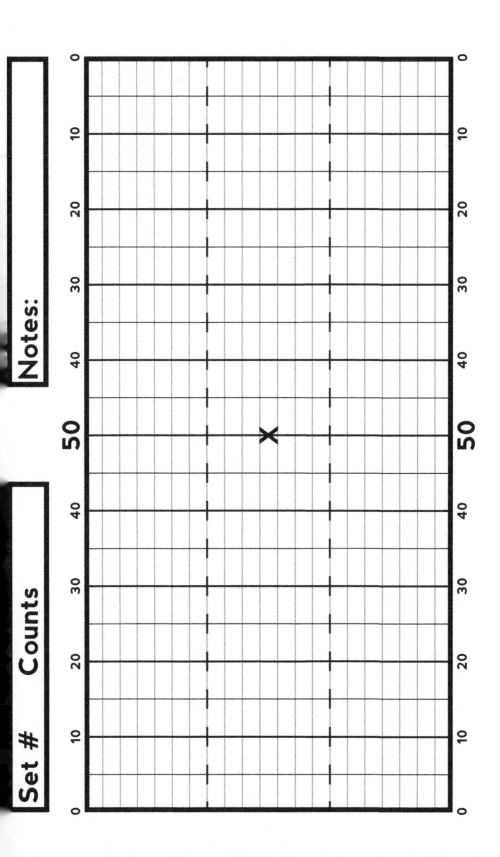

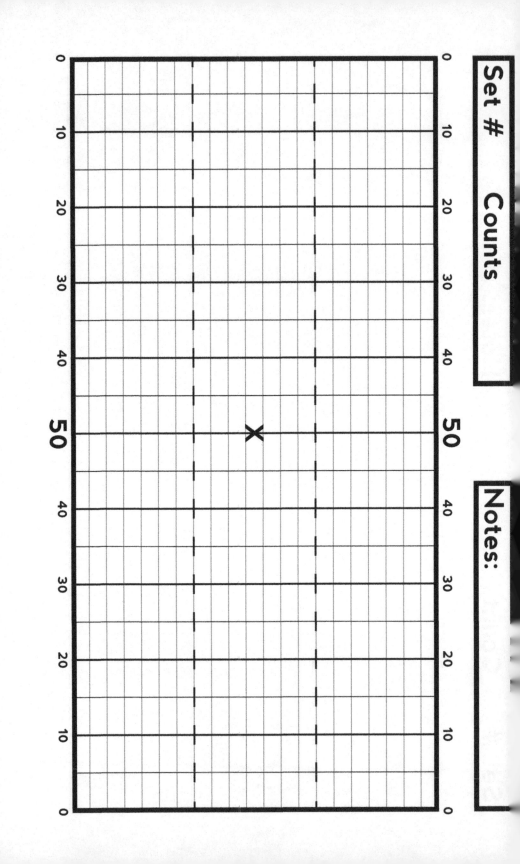

Set #   Counts

Notes:

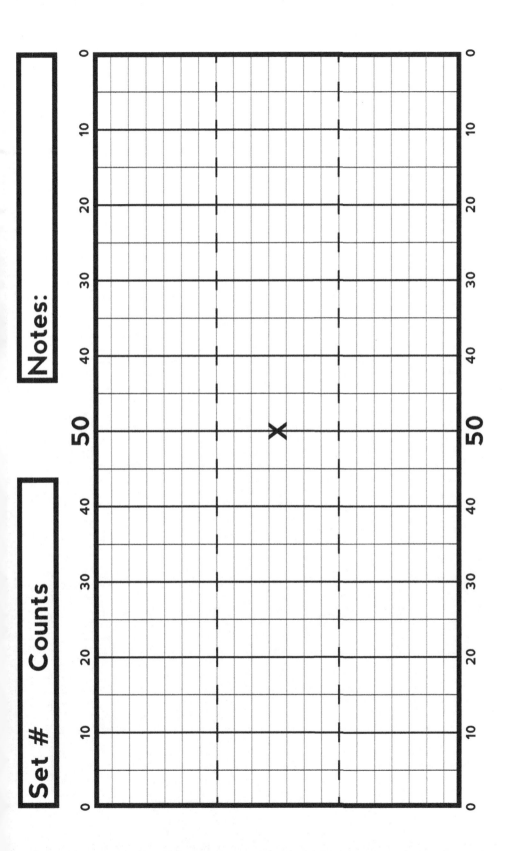

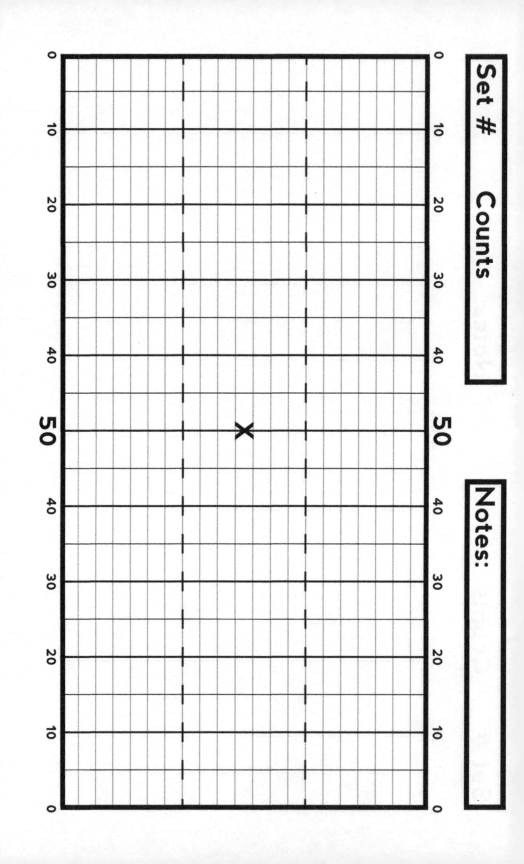

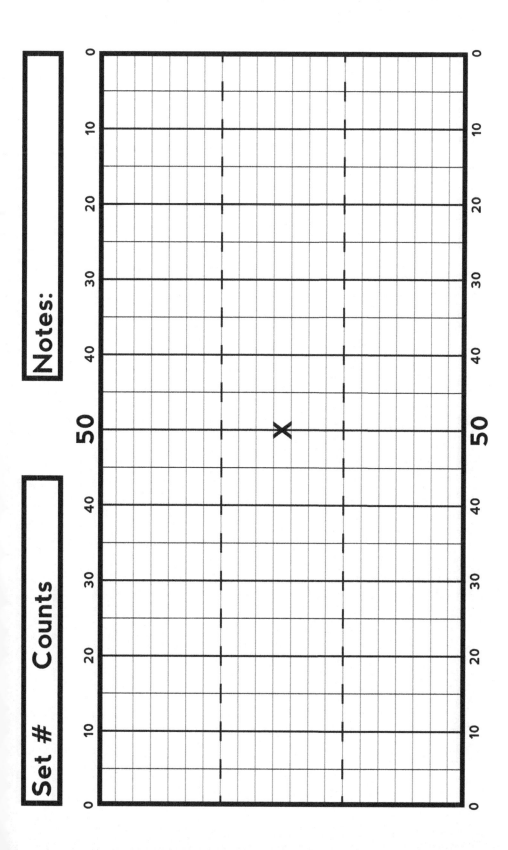

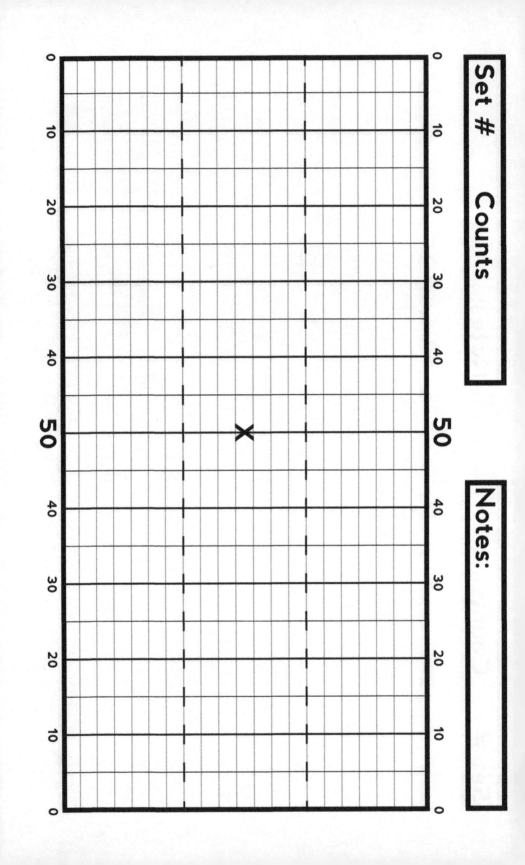

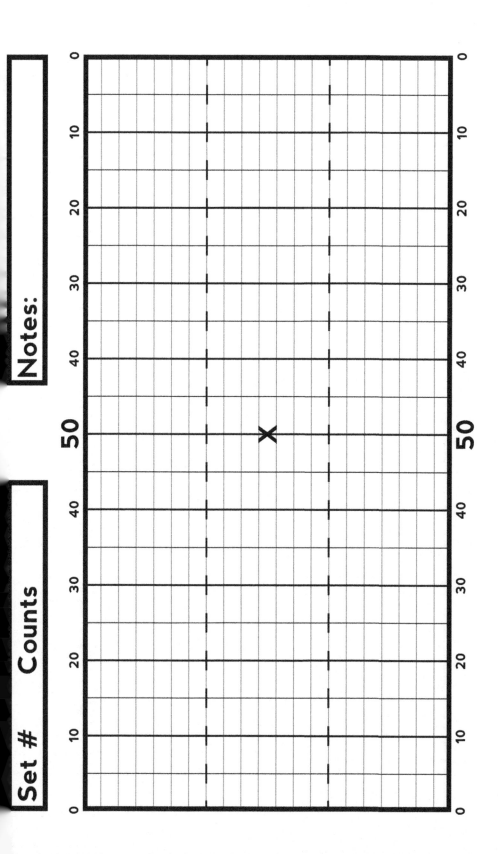

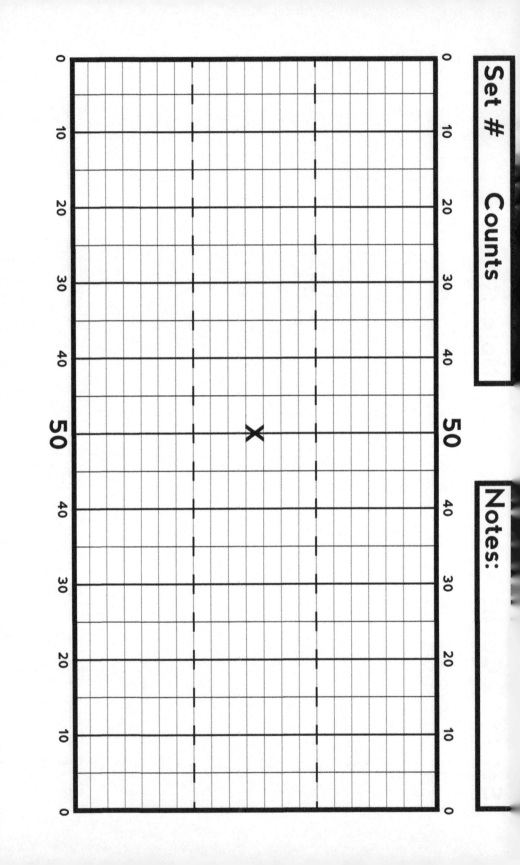

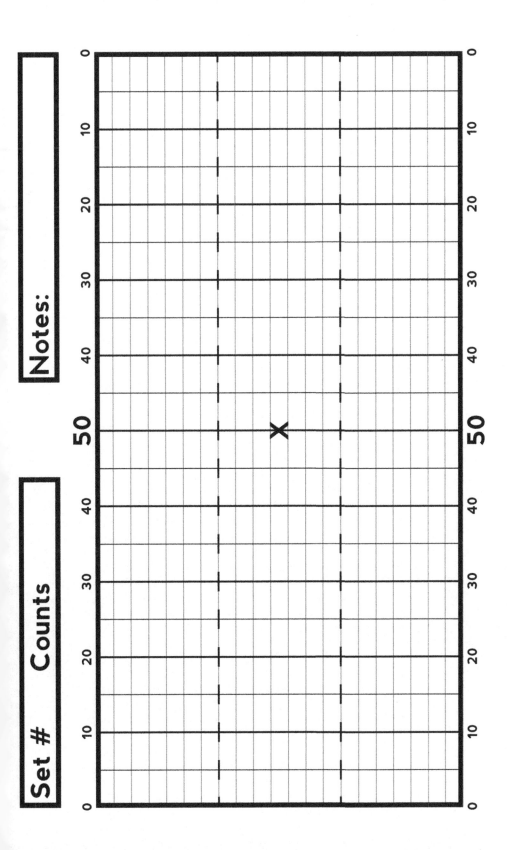

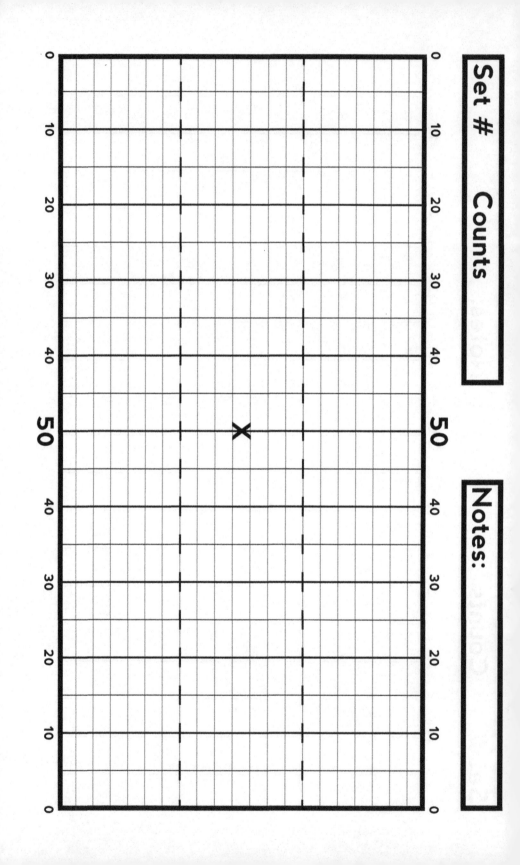

Notes:

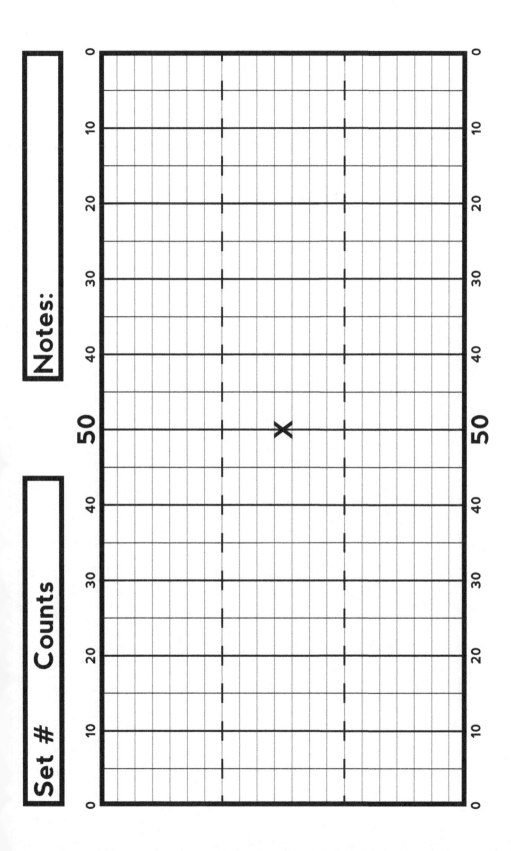

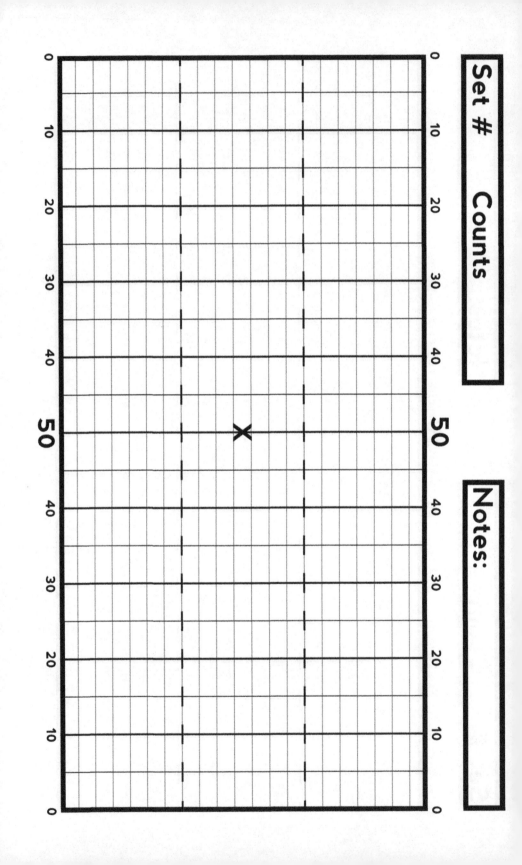

Set #   Counts   Notes:

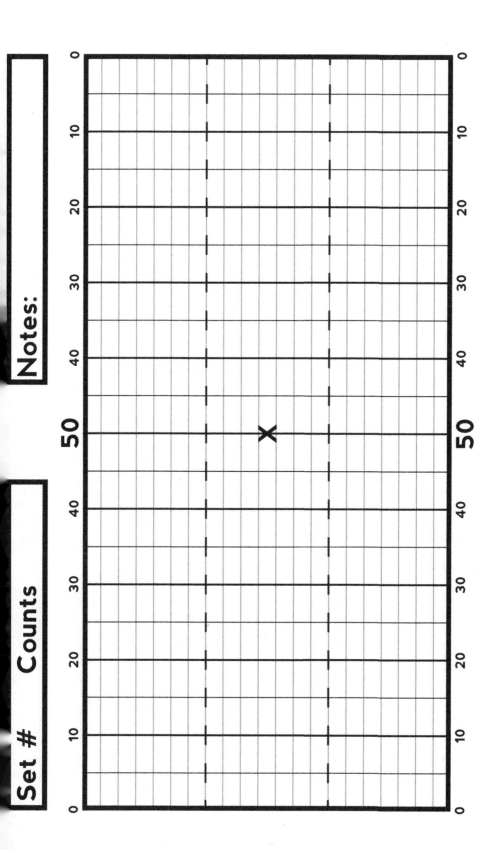

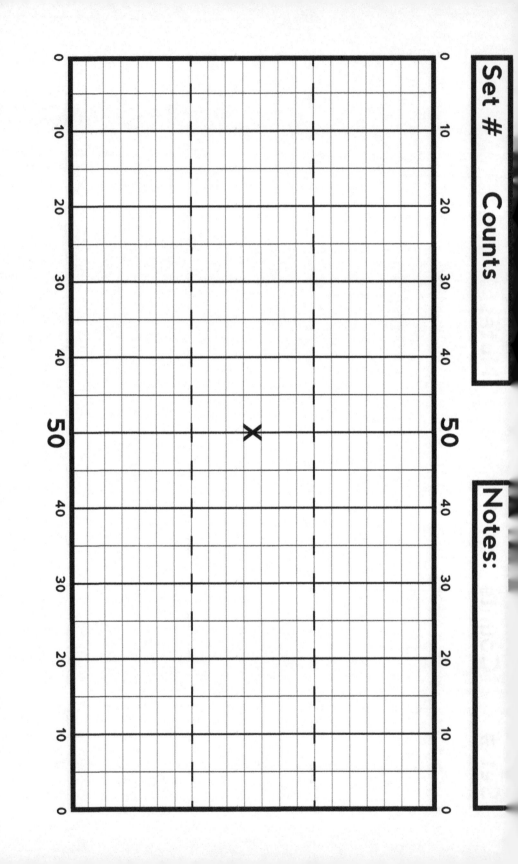

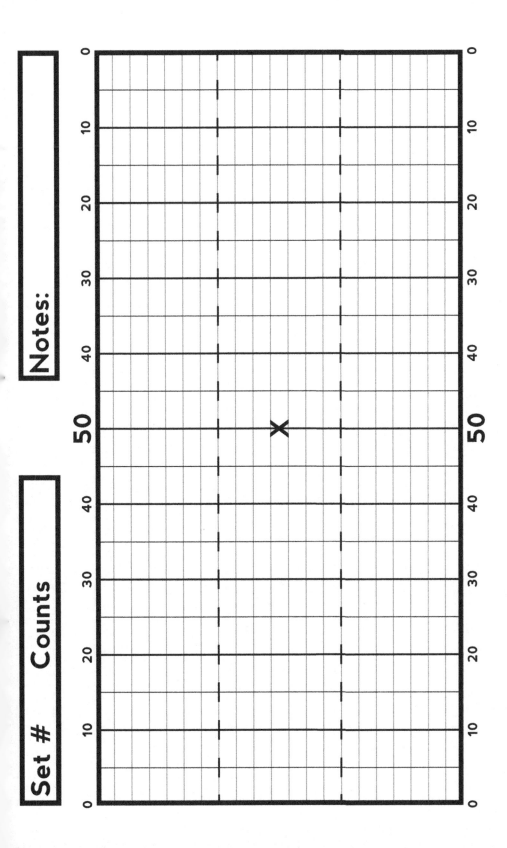

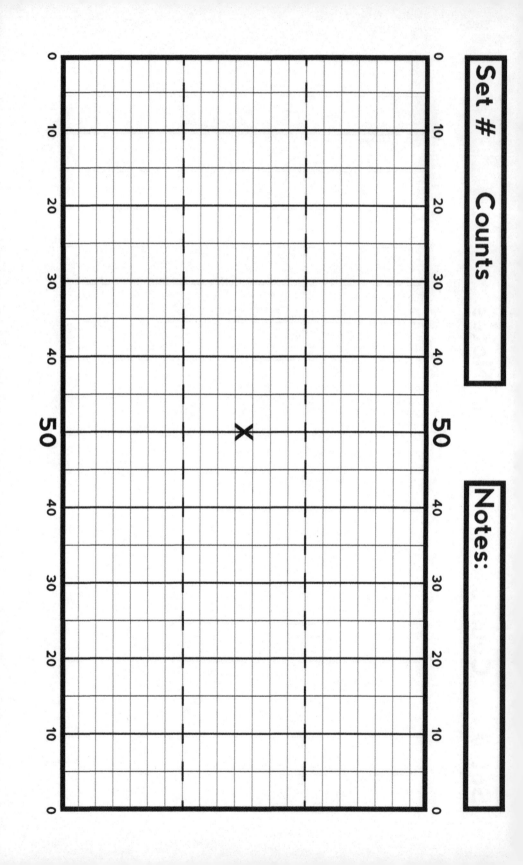

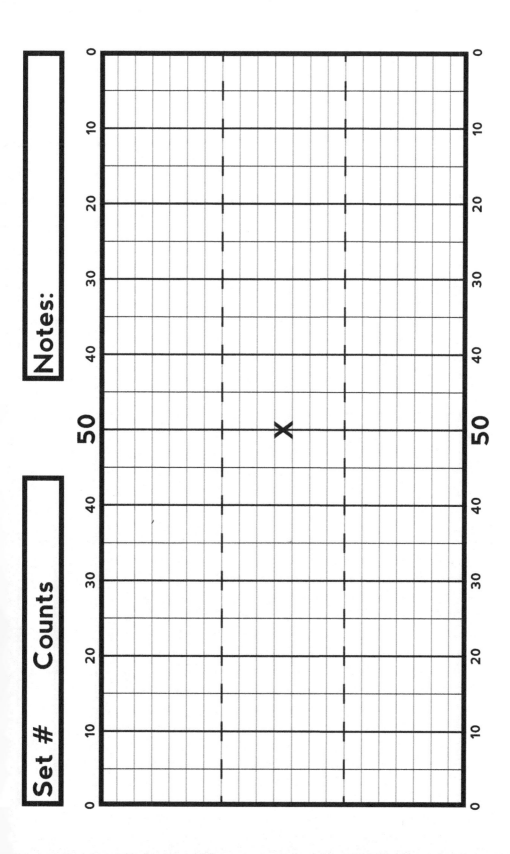

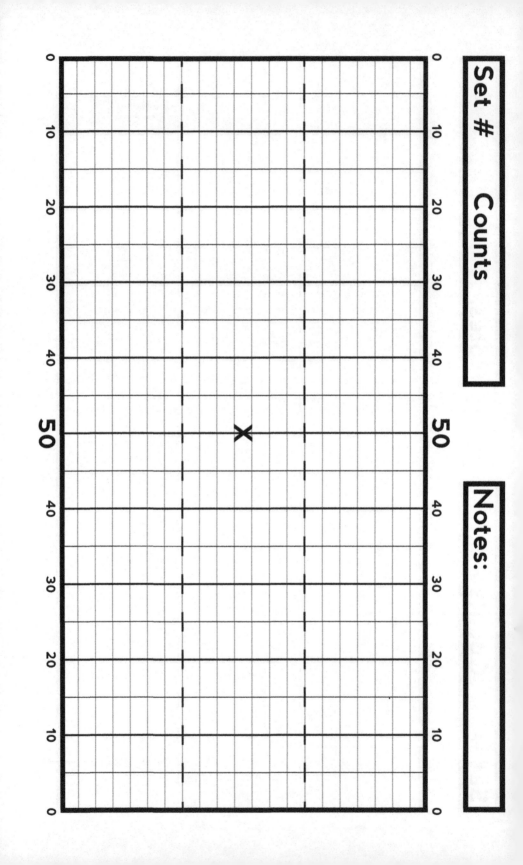

Set #   Counts

Notes:

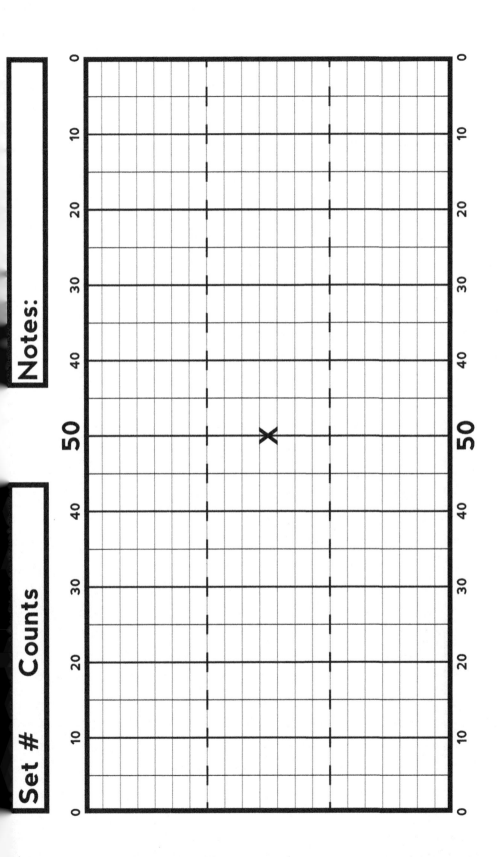

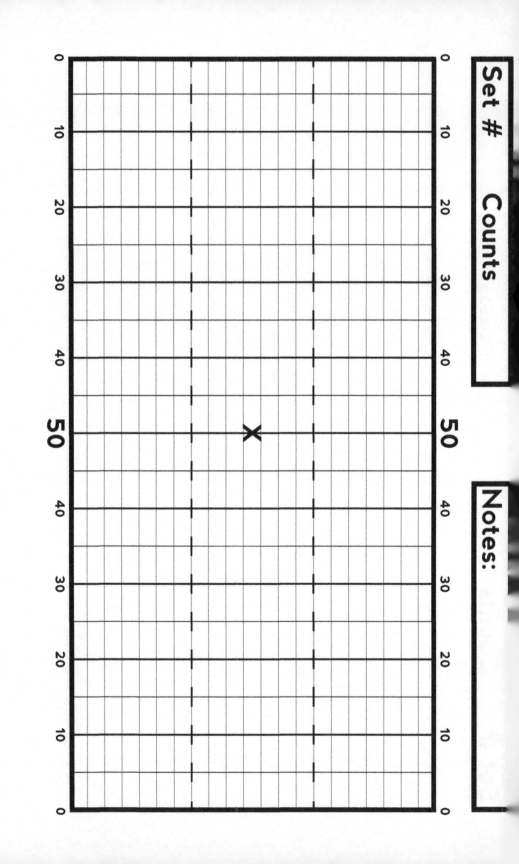

Made in United States
North Haven, CT
10 July 2022

21145593R00075